NOW, YO[...]
"AS DANGER[...]
WITH AN ELEPHANT GUN."*

"A SPOOFY, GOOFY TREATISE that includes everything from a letter alerting the Secretary of Defense to this cheap-yet-allegedly effective weapons systems to the techniques behind tossing cards through the air with the greatest of ease."
—*Chicago Daily News*

"AN ESSENTIAL HANDBOOK FOR THE URBAN DWELLER."
—*Newsday*

"EVEN IF YOU HAVE NO INTEREST AT ALL IN FLIPPING CARDS, YOU'LL STILL ENJOY THIS BOOK. In addition, the volume contains complete instructions—clearly illustrated—on how to become a card tosser of Olympic caliber . . . within a few short months, you'll be ready to face a sneering rhino or charging wino with equal nonchalance." —*Circus* **magazine**

"DECK-DEFYING . . . ostensibly a straightforward study of how ordinary playing cards can be used to ward off muggers, slay wild animals or remove a spleen . . . a cosmic spoof of the How-To genre." —*Los Angeles Times*

"DELIGHTFUL . . . with a Pepys-like frankness Ricky Jay dispels any sceptic's thoughts on the validity of throwing playing cards as a martial art form of self-defense . . . presents a rich embroiling history of the art of card throwing along with in-depth methods." —*The Grapevine Press*

"A MOST AMUSING BOOK." —*San Francisco Chronicle*

Die Transvaler, a South African newspaper, when describing Jay's card-throwing feats.

CARDS
—AS—
WEAPONS

Ricky Jay

WARNER BOOKS

A Warner Communications Company

Warner Books Edition

Copyright © 1977 by Ricky Jay

This Warner Books edition is published by arrangement
with the author

Warner Books, Inc., 666 Fifth Avenue, New York, NY 10103

w A Warner Communications Company

Printed in the United States of America

First Warner Books Printing: June 1988

10 9 8 7 6 5 4 3 2 1

Library of Congress Cataloging-in-Publication Data

Jay, Ricky
  Cards as weapons / Ricky Jay.
     p. cm.
  Originally published: New York : Darien Books, c1977.
  1. Card tricks—Anecdotes, facetiae, satire, etc. I. Title.
[GV1549.J28 1988]
795.4′38′0207—dc19   87-28956
  ISBN 0-446-38756-8 (pbk.)(U.S.A.)
  ISBN 0-446-38755X (pbk.)(Canada)

Designed by Giorgetta Bell McRee
Cover design by William Graef
Cover illustration by Steve Macanga
based on original hardcover
jacket illustration by
Gary Cooley

For
KEN BROOKE, whom I greatly admire as an
artist, entertainer, and human being;

and for
MAX KATZ, my grandfather, who taught me,
and taught me what to look for.

A treatise on the art of throwing, scaling, juggling, boomeranging, and manipulating ordinary playing cards with particular emphasis on impressing one's friends and providing a deadly yet inexpensive means of self-defense.

In which the author recounts with clarity and excessive exaggeration how he has helped the elderly, abetted the police, and assuaged the plight of young damsels with the help of his trusty cards.

A sad footnote. The death by suicide of a San Quentin inmate who blew himself to a netherworld with a bomb fashioned from a pack of cards. For those who doubt the seriousness of the subject or the tone of the tome.

*On a pleasant, breezy day
a short while ago, a letter of
great significance was received
by the Secretary of Defense.*

*The letter is reproduced
on the following page.*

*The plausibility of this idea
and its importance to each and
every citizen is the subject
of this book.*

Columbia School of Card Throwing

37 RIVERSIDE DRIVE, NEW YORK, N.Y. 10023

Ricky Jay, President

Date: 31 May 1976

SUBJECT: Martial Projectiles

TO: The Honorable Secretary of Defense
             The Pentagon
             Washington, D.C.

    1.   I have spent the last ten years actively engaged in researching and analyzing the military applications of the ordinary playing card.

    2.   Drawing on techniques used hundreds of years ago by "ninja" assassins, I have developed my own system of self-defense based solely on a pack of cards.

    3.   I have simplified the techniques to a degree where they could be taught to our servicemen in a matter of weeks. I would be willing to go to Fort Dix in Nutley, New Jersey to give a demonstration of these skills. My cousin Stanley Felber was stationed there some years ago and when I visited him I found the camp quite pleasant although the goldenrod did bother my rather sensitive sniffer just a little.

    4.   Currently there is widespread concern about our economy; fiduciary matters are on the tip of everyone's tongue. I believe I have discovered a viable method of reducing the national Defense budget while keeping a few steps ahead of the Russkies.

    5.   I have also given thought to the serious problem of peacetime morale and am convinced that playing cards could do a great deal to solace and uplift our men before an actual attack.

    Please do not misconstrue my meaning; I of course abhor the evil of gambling and the onanistic pleasures of solitaire. I have, however, discovered that the deck of cards can serve one as Bible, Prayer Book, and Almanac:

(a) The Ace reminds us that there is but one God;
the Deuce of the Father and Son; the Trey of
the Holy Trinity; the Four reminds us of Matthew,
Mark, Luke and John; the Five of the five wise
and five foolish virgins; the Six stands for the
six days in which the world was made; the Seven
for the seventh day on which He rested; Eight
reminds us of the eight good people saved from
the Flood; the Nine of the nine lepers whom the
Lord cleansed; the Ten of the Ten Commandments;
the Jack of Jack Anderson who in the next world
shall suffer the fate of all infidels; the Queen
of the Queen of Sheba and hence the wisdom of
Solomon; and the King is the Creator — the King
of All.

(b) The three-hundred-and-sixty-five days of the
year are shown by the total number of spots in
the deck; the fifty-two weeks by the number of
cards; the four seasons by the four suits; and
day and night are represented by the red and
black cards.

So you see, Mr. Honorable Secretary, the cards can serve
as Bible, Prayer Book, and Almanac, thus providing a deadly yet
inexpensive means of self-defense.

6.   It would be unwise to further elucidate the subject
of this missive for fear the information would fall into the
wrong hands.

7.   I am awaiting your reply so that a meeting may be
arranged at our mutual convenience.

Ricky Jay

RICKY JAY
President and
Pasteboard Projectilist

Ricky Jay

A brief account of the origins of playing cards with some subtle speculation as to when they were first thrown.

History

A Lobster

Divinatory Arrows

To determine the inventor of the playing card is as difficult as determining who ate the first lobster. And if it was a very hungry man who wrestled that bizarre crustacean to his mouth, so it must have been a very bored man who fashioned the precursor to the card by carving symbols on a stick or stone.

Noted scholars have suggested that both cards and chess were derived from the arrow. In fact, divinatory systems with the arrow are frequently cited as the basis of *all* games, as well as the classification of all things. The entire structure or order of known things, in almost every ancient culture, was based on the Four Directions expressed by crossed arrows. All things not shown in this obvious scheme of things were considered different, hence magical. It seems that from the very earliest times, the roots of cards lay in both the mystical and martial thoughts of man.

Picture, if you will, a single card, inscribed with a magical prayer, hurled through the air with the speed and accuracy of the mighty arrow. Whish! Swat! Swoosh! Thwack! And a hated adversary stumbles, desperately clutching his furrowed brow, where that card, that weapon, has become implanted. *Watch now: a spurt of blood, and the insidious foe crashes thunderously to the ground! The day is won. The city is saved. And the weapon, the use of the mighty card, is seen as a natural evolution of a process with its roots in all antiquity!*

Excuse me.

These systems of arrow divination were integral to the peoples of ancient China, Korea, Egypt, Persia, and the American Indians. At some time in the dim past arrows gave way to gaming sticks, pebbles, and what we now call dice. Soon thereafter symbols

Proof of the existence of cards as weapons during the Viking invasion of North America.

Further proof

*Ricky Jay and Professor Carl Sagan of Cornell
University and Jet Propulsion Laboratories
discuss trajectory of thrown cards and the
possibility of throwing cards on Mars.*

were marked by hand on strips of paper and
playing cards were born.

And if it is difficult to trace the origins of the
playing card, it is equally difficult to speculate
as to where or when the first card game was
played; or at what point mysticism gave way
to idle pleasure, mathematical diversion, or
gambling skill.

Realizing, however, that we are inclined to
believe that all peoples who preceded us were
savages, we can no doubt assume that shortly
after the first card game, an enigmatic Egyp-
tian, inscrutable Oriental, or self-righteous
Hindu picked up the pack of cards and
clouted his more successful partner over the
head with them.

It is this moment, difficult to document but
sure to exist, about which we are curious.

The major documentary studies of weapons
seem to overlook cards in much the same way
our contemporaries overlook the beauty of a
rich thick fog. As the accompanying evolutionary chart will show, playing cards have
their proper place in the developmental sequence of martial projectiles.

There is little doubt that cards are one of the
earliest of impractical weapons.

The Evolutionary
Chart of Weaponry

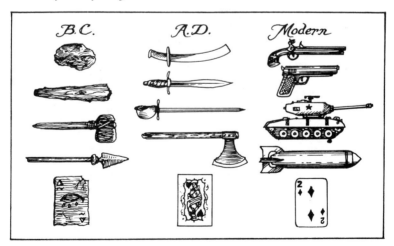

*A reflective look at the
shuriken and other deadly
throwing weapons of the
venerable Orientals with a
lucid parallel to the
modern card assassin.*

Cards
And The
Martial
Arts

The Horse-and-Carriage

Ham-and-Eggs

Buck-and-Wing

Cards and the martial arts may be coupled in the same fashion as many of the most famous pairs in American song and food: the horse-and-carriage, the ham-and-egg, the buck-and-wing.

The martial arts have always stressed spiritual control based on physical and mental accomplishments. Cards lend themselves wonderfully well to this process. In the right hands, cards will become a meditative tool similar to the Indian mantra, and the esthetic pleasure in holding and feeling a deck of cards cannot be denied. One can become so relaxed and engrossed with the cards that he may soon be transported to another world; such is the special power of the pasteboards.

Dai Vernon, the dean of American magicians (and, in this author's opinion, the greatest living contributor to the magical art), has said that cards are like living breathing human beings and should be treated accordingly.

Tomes have been written on the divinatory and predictive powers of the cards and from their earliest history to the present day, many people have made this study their life's work.

These concepts may be more readily fathomed by the Eastern mind. In fact, to paraphrase an ancient parable, he who masters his art (be it karate, the tea ceremony or the handling of cards), masters the art of life.

It is, therefore, necessary to trace the origins of cards and card-like devices used in self-defense before a complete understanding of our subject may be reached.

The ancient Chinese and Japanese have documented the origins and use of many classical weapons and it is best to start our study with these.

E.T.C. Werner, H.B.M. Consul, Foochow

(retired), Barrister-At-Law, Middle Temple, and Member of the Chinese Government Historiographical Bureau in Peking, wrote the classic English work on Chinese weaponry in 1932. *Chinese Weapons,* Werner's book, was recently republished in the United States (Ohara Publications, Los Angeles, 1972). The book deals with the origins and use of Chinese weapons. Though Mr. Werner limits in large part his discussions of hand-thrown weapons to spear-like devices, he makes some observations which are relevant or at least interesting enough to be mentioned. Werner traces the origin of iron caltrops, devices which look like children's jacks, but with highly sharpened points. These were thrown in the path of pursuing foes and were an effective deterrent. The ninja or "invisible assassins" of Japan used these caltrops which they called *tetsu-bishi* but Werner finds them mentioned in the time of Emperor Wen Ti (179–156 B.C.) and the Emperor places their origin at a much earlier period.

The use of the caltrop is the forerunner to a self-defense technique called "Springing the Cards." A deck of cards is held with thumb on the bottom edge and all the fingers along the top in the cupped right hand. The cards are bent until they are under great pressure and then are released directly at an assailant's face; they leap out in a confusing spray giving the dealer ample time to escape.

Springing the Cards

Crossbows invented by the Chinese around 2600 B.C. came to be made in a variety of materials and designs. Some of the earliest wooden models used to launch arrows bear a marked similarity to a product called Zing-It, marketed by one R.A. Hamilton of Plainfield, New Jersey. Mr. Hamilton is also the inventor of Whippersnapper, Zoomerang and Mr. Molasses. We will discuss Mr. Hamilton's product at some length in the chapter dealing with mechanical devices, but for the moment it will suffice to say that Zing-It is a crossbow-like T-shaped piece of wood which propels a playing card a considerable distance.

Werner also mentions a secret weapon named *hsien-chien* "which caused death when hurled at an enemy's forehead." To this the author adds his own subtle conjectures: first, that this weapon is a rectangular piece of thin metal very similar to a playing card; and second, that it required *hitting* the enemy's forehead to cause injury, let alone death.

Another weapon thrown by the ancient Chinese was a large jar filled with the whites of goose and duck eggs mixed with the oil of the dryandra tree. This was thrown on the deck of attacking war vessels, the combination of the pieces of the bottle and the incredibly slippery solution making it difficult for the sailors to keep their footing. The solution was flammable and when sparked by fire arrows it caused the vessel to ignite. "Possibly," says Mr. Werner, "this was the prototype of the stinkpot. . . ."

The ninja mentioned briefly a short while ago were one of the most amazing groups of men ever assembled. Originating in Japan during the reign of the Empress Suiko (593–628 A.D.), their early work was as secret agents gathering information for civil actions. They grew to be an incredible group of almost superhuman spies and assassins. By the thirteenth century the art of ninjutsu or "stealing in" had been developed to include proficiency in the use of almost all the weapons and martial arts of the day.

Ninja were trained from childhood in all methods of self-defense in addition to such special skills as muscular and breath control (especially under water), disguise, acting, concealment, medicine and pharmacology. According to *Ninja, The Invisible Assassins* (Ohara Publications, Los Angeles, 1970) by Andrew Adams, "The ninja was a superb escape artist who would have made Houdini look like a rank amateur. He could dislocate his joints at will to slip out complicated knots. He hid in bells, above ceilings, under floors, remained under water by breathing through reeds and tobacco pipes, concealed himself in trees and wells and even disguised himself as a rock or tree stump. In fact, this ability to appear unobtrusive and disappear into the surrounding scenery was what probably gave rise to the tales that the ninja could make himself disappear at will. It should come as no surprise then that ninjutsu has been defined as the 'art of invisibility'."

Here then is something for every would-be conjurer to think about.

One of the ninja's chief weapons was the shuriken, a flat sharp pointed object of metal that came in a variety of shapes and sizes. There were at least ten different types of shuriken; the five-pointed star and four-pointed or card-shaped were the most common. Great amounts of time were spent in learning to throw these articles from unusual positions and with a minimum of arm motion. It was also important to be able to hurl the shuriken while running at top speed. The expert could throw them into dime-size targets at distances of up to thirty-five feet.

Though the ninja were banned by the Tokugawa Shogunate in the seventeenth cen-

Shuriken

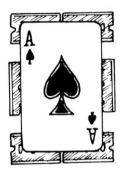

A Razor-Bladed Card

tury, their methods have intrigued scholars and students of the martial arts to this day. Some martial arts supply houses carry a sort of deck of thin rectangular shuriken which are held in the left hand and flipped outward by a sharp pressure of the right thumb against the back of the metal. Care must be taken to see that the right thumb does not hit the edge of the metal which is extremely sharp. With the proper stroke, an incredible repeating action can be mastered and a number of steel cards sent flying in less than a second.

This parallels a modern card propelling method used by the very inventive Dutch conjurer "Flip." He places his extended right forefinger flush against the center of the pack which is held firmly in the left hand. By moving the forefinger sharply forward and creating friction against the rest of the pack, the top card is propelled forward with surprising speed and velocity.

Many present-day scalawags have taken ordinary playing cards and inserted razor blades strategically around the edges. This makeshift tool of terror can cause great harm, but so too can a large stick in adept hands. Unless experts are using this technique there is little to fear.

The use of poison-coated cards is nearly as ancient as the cards themselves. Over the years many substances have been used to hasten the demise of princes and peasants alike. There is no time to explain all these toxins but the author will discuss what is, in his opinion, the most effective of these terminal additives.

First, get a blowfish. Not just any blowfish, but one of the poisonous variety. The cognoscenti will use only the *fugu* fish found primarily in the Sea of Japan. This fish possesses a poison called *tetrodotoxin* which adds verisimilitude to an otherwise bald and unconvincing fish. This poison, like the curare employed by the Jivaro Indians of South America, produces its deleterious effects by a paralysis of the central nervous system (CNS), death usually occurring by suffocation as the respiratory apparatus gasps to a halt. This poison may be spread on playing cards (the specific quantity and method of application have been omitted from this manuscript at the request of certain Agencies) and if the flesh is pierced death supervenes within five minutes.

Jivaro Indian

Specially licensed Japanese chefs are permitted to prepare the poison-tinged flesh of the blowfish for human consumption. Only enough poison remains to give the piscatorial gourmet or Yakuza Sammy Glick an intoxication in his epicurean Russian roulette.

A Blowfish

The use of lethal cards by modern-day hit men has of course been hushed by the authorities.

Training camps for these paid assassins exist frequently right under the noses of those most eager to learn of them. Some have tried to exploit the author's knowledge of such but his lips are sealed both by honor and constitutional privilege. These highly secret installations have been in operation for years; Sun Tzu mentions them in his essays on the art of war (about 400 B.C.). Further information is available in documents entrusted to the Miskatonic University Library in Arkham, Massachusetts.

Mastery of multiple weapons is essential to the modern-day mercenary and he would no more think of overlooking cards than catgut.

Every now and then a story will appear in a

small-town newspaper about a sinister look-ing outlander apprehended with his violin case containing only cards, but in this frenetic day and age such events go largely unnoted.

In the movie *Goldfinger* the character Odd-job is able to decapitate statues and even unapotheosized flesh with the toss of a steel-brimmed hat.

A hat, indeed!

Ian Fleming spent years as an intelligence officer and knew full well what the real weapon was. (Devotees of the 007 series will recall that James Bond was apparently done in by the aforementioned poison of the *fugu* fish in the closing pages of *From Russia With Love.*)

It is impossible to write a chapter on the martial arts without mentioning the late Bruce Lee.

SETTING THE WORLD RECORD IN LONDON

In November of 1976, Ricky Jay was flown to London to appear on the Michael Parkinson Christmas Special for BBC-TV. At that time Mr. Norris McWhirter, Editor of the Guinness Book of World Records and representatives of three London newspapers were invited to watch Mr. Jay demonstrate his unique skills with playing cards. That visit resulted in a new world record and subsequent entry in the Guiness Book of World Records.

Jay hurls cards through London dailies at speeds estimated over 90 m.p.h. Holding the "Mail" is Norris McWhirter.

Michael Parkinson and Norris McWhirter prepare for the brutal card onslaught.

Jay demonstrates accuracy by throwing card into small window at BBC Studios.

Jay in front of BBC Studios . . . all in a day's work.

Historical accounts of the scaling of cards into the far reaches of small theaters. A feat of skill included in the stage shows of famous magicians, with particular emphasis on Herrmann the Great and the Amazing Thurston.

Magicians And Card-Scaling

The act of throwing cards as a demonstration of skill must be included in any serious history of stage magic in this country. Yet, with the exception of this author's interest, and his demonstration of such, it is a skill rarely if ever seen today.

Two of America's greatest magicians, Alexander Herrmann and Howard Thurston, made the scaling of cards into the audience a feature of their performances.

Alexander Herrmann, fondly remembered by old-timers (he died in 1896) as Herrmann the Great, was the most famous of a dynasty of wonderful performers.

His father was Dr. Samuel Herrmann who, in addition to his work as a surgeon, was performing magic on the Continent for such notables as the Sultan of Turkey and even Napoleon. He also found time to sire sixteen children. The eldest, Carl, born in 1816, left medical school for the life of a wandering wizard, and by all accounts was one of the most skilled to join the profession. It is interesting to note that Carl's first successes were in the field of bird imitations.

Alexander, who was twenty-seven years younger than Carl, first joined the elder's show for a command performance for the Czar of Russia in 1853. It seems that Alexander's departure was not announced to the Doctor, who could not bear the thought of his youngest son also passing up medicine for the sordid life of a sorcerer. He supposedly threatened to bring kidnapping charges against Carl unless Alexander was returned.

The threat—in fact the use of police intervention to dampen the enthusiasm of would-be conjurers—is an attempted deterrent which is still prevalent. This author's personal

Alexander Herrmann

experiences, as well as those of the Seldom-
Seen Kid and other magic notables, will in due
course be revealed; but this is hardly the place
for such pulpy gems.

At any rate, Alexander's skill supposedly
softened the Doctor's calloused exterior and
he allowed the child to continue under Carl's
tutelage.

Alexander eventually presented his own
show, playing mostly in the United States,
while Carl remained on the Continent. It is
not known exactly when Alexander intro-
duced the scaling of cards into his show, but
there is no doubt that it became one of the
features of his act. At the height of his career,
when Alexander was both the wealthiest and
best-known performer in America, he threw
thousands and thousands of thin cardboard
cards, decorated with his picture and signa-
ture, into theater galleries around the country.

A considerable portion of Alexander's great
reputation came from his impromptu performances. While walking down a street or
dining in a restaurant he would take advantage of any situation that would evoke laugh-
ter or garner free publicity. He would apparently find gold pieces in fruit just purchased
from a street vendor or he would extract the
watch from a bystander's pocket while being
observed by a policeman. When Alexander
was dragged to the police station the watch
would be found in the policeman's pocket
rather than his own. Once, at the famous
Whitechapel Club in Chicago, Alexander attempted to throw a card into a small opening
at the juncture of the woodwork lining and
the ceiling. He took two entire packs of cards
and threw them unsuccessfully until a single
card remained in his hand. Then, glancing

slyly about, he took the card and with a faultless throw lodged it perfectly in the crack. There it remained until the Club ceased to exist.

Although Alexander was unquestionably a great showman and skilled performer, he was not noted for his creativity as a magician, and many of his effects were copied from DeKolta, Maskelyne, and other notable performers of his day. So it was with his card-throwing; though not original, it became his trademark. His skill and accuracy made it a spectacular event; he started an American magical tradition.

Howard Thurston

Howard Thurston was born in 1869. His first significant job was as a newspaper boy on the trains that passed through Columbus, Ohio, on their way to Akron and Pittsburgh.

Young Howard saw playbills advertising Herrmann the Great and saved his pennies until he was able to buy the most inexpensive ticket, high in the balcony, for Herrmann's final show in Columbus. (Or so the legend goes, and magic legends being almost as simplistic as most magicians, who are we to argue?)

Needless to say, Howard was inspired. We can even conjecture that Howard caught one of the souvenir cards Herrmann threw into the gallery and that, since the wrist action in throwing both cards and folded newspapers is identical, Howard soon became proficient at throwing cards.

In any event, that inspiration soon gave way to another, no, to *the* other inspiration. Thurston soon enrolled in Mt. Hermon School as a medical missionary. After completing his studies he decided to enroll in medical school at the University of Pennsylvania. It was in

the Albany, New York, train station, with
Howard en route from Columbus to Philadel-
phia early in 1892, that the second legend-
making incident took place. While waiting for
the connecting train Thurston saw an advertisement for the Herrmann show. Remember-
ing his earlier inspiration he stayed over to see
it and was once again awestricken. It was
Herrmann's last night in Albany and, when
Howard appeared at the railway station in the
morning, the master magician and his wife
were at the ticket window inquiring about the
next train to Syracuse. For the rest of this
spine-tingling tale I must quote from Walter
Gibson's *The Master Magicians* (Doubleday,
New York, 1966):

"Howard heard the ticket agent say '8:20'
and as Herrmann turned away, Howard
pushed a twenty-dollar bill through the window, saying he wanted a ticket to Philadel-
phia. Back it came, with the change, but as
Howard glanced at the ticket he saw that it
read 'Syracuse.' It was already 8:15 and an an-
nouncer was calling 'All aboard for Syracuse!'
Howard saw the Hermanns going through the
train gate; on impulse he followed them and
boarded it.

"That incident shaped the career of Howard
Thurston. In Syracuse he attended Herrmann's opening performance and was even
more fascinated than in Albany the night
before. His mind was made up; he would
become a magician, not a missionary."

As sad as this story may be to all devoted to
spreading the Word, we may all take heart in
the fact that while few men are as successful
as those they try to emulate, Howard Thurston did become the most successful and best-
known magician in America.

Though known in his later years for a huge illusion show (at one time ten railroad baggage cars were needed to transport his props) his reputation was originally made by his skill with cards; card-throwing was a major feature of his act. Like Herrmann, Thurston threw thousands of good luck cards into the outstretched hands of eager fans throughout the country.

Amazingly enough, many of magic's most famous old-time performers threw souvenir cards into theatre galleries.

More than a hundred years ago, Robert-Houdin, the incredible French conjurer, wrote about card-throwing and mentioned seeing a Hungarian performer named Well who threw a card and had it boomerang back to his hand. Robert-Houdin also mentioned that card-throwing was a useful skill because it allowed one to distribute small books or souvenirs to the audience via the same basic method. "Once," he says, "I threw one of the little sketchbooks from my horn of plenty, right across the chandelier to the spectators in the upper gallery, and gained tremendous applause for the boldness of the feat."

Early in his career Houdini, the famous escape artist, was billed as "The King of Cards," and he too was proficient at throwing and boomeranging cards. Occasionally, as a card returned to him, he would lunge forward and with a pair of scissors cut it neatly in half.

The great French performers Felicien Trewey and Jean Valton, both highly skilled at card flourishes and throwing tricks, used them to make their reputations. Mehay, mentioned in Sachs' *Sleight of Hand* (1875), would put a card on the back of his left hand and flick it into the audience with his right forefinger.

Frederick Eugene Powell, the late Dean of the
Society of American Magicians, threw cards,
as did Will Rock, one of Thurston's successors.
More recently a performer named Benjamin
Franklin IV did an entire vaudeville act based
on card-throwing, and currently Flip and
Richard Ross of Holland, Finn Jon of Norway,
Christian of Vienna, and Whitey Roberts in
the United States have all included clever card
throwing techniques in their acts.

Most performers threw cards made of a
cardboard stock heavier than the ordinary
playing card and consequently easier to
throw. These cards were generally embla-
zoned with the picture and autograph of the
magician, and often bore some greeting such
as "Luck to You." These were valuable advertising pieces for the performer and today are
eagerly sought by collectors of antique mag-
icana.

Sometime during the years of the Second
World War card-throwing was withdrawn
from popular view and its secrets covetously
guarded and performed by only a chosen few.
It may well be that the American cultural
conscience found it too wily, too Oriental a
means of expression to be comfortably coun-
tenanced. Perhaps it was rationing, and all
that it entails, or the war effort itself which
left Americans with no time to develop this
specialty. Still another possibility was the lack
of good instructional material by highly qual-
ified teachers.

The author, fortunate enough to have acquired these special skills and to have added a
few ideas of his own, is honored in being able
to continue this recondite tradition. He sin-
cerely hopes his readers will succeed him in
this formerly exclusive coterie.

The basics of card-throwing (illustrated): the Herrmann method, the Thurston method, and the Jay method. The hand, the wrist, the grip, and the all-important follow-through.

Technique

It may interest the reader or—if he is a strange fellow—excite him to learn that this is far from the first written discussion concerning the technique of throwing playing cards. In the author's files are more than fifty references to throwing, spinning, boomeranging and dealing cards and the different magical effects which may be done with these techniques.

The bulk of these may be found in now-defunct magician's periodicals and out-of-print books. The author is well aware of the risk he is taking by tackling this subject; his publisher is nearly suicidal.

Magical literature, like the magical art, is overrun with misinformation and redundancies; there is little of practical value. In magic, as in most ancient arts, the oral tradition still provides the best method for learning. Characteristically, it is the unpublished material, merely spoken of or held covetously by a chosen few, that houses the truly great secrets of the noble art.

The trend toward the popularization of magic through the publication of previously select and guarded methods will do little or nothing to lift the art from the miasmic murk which has surrounded it for years. Nor will it be improved by the general availability of magical secrets and effects pitched by former used-car salesmen in their antiseptic glass-enclosed cages, surrounded by guillotines and arm-choppers and halves of ladies with fringe and teased blonde hair, combined with the public appearances of those persons too ill-equipped to perform for even the most boring family reunions.

This is merely the author's rationalization for writing the book. After twenty years of the pain inflicted on him by witnessing poor card

tricks, a tome which explains how cards are
used to inflict pain is not only fitting but
spiritually justifiable.

> *Do you like card tricks? he asked.*
> *I said no.*
> *He did five.*
> *—W. Somerset Maugham*

Since Herrmann and Thurston were the
most famous of the card-throwers we will
commence with a discussion of their methods.

An article comparing these two gentlemen,
with accompanying illustrations, was published in a 1936 edition of the *Sphinx* magic
magazine. Quoted is the part which discusses
their techniques.

"It is particularly interesting that Howard
Thurston and Alexander Herrmann did not
perform the feat in the same way. They both
used cards of much heavier stock than the
ordinary playing card. This gave the cards
added weight which permitted them to be
thrown much farther than the standard playing cards could be thrown. Howard Thurston
gripped one end of the card between his first
and second fingers and threw it by a snap of
his wrist. Herrmann gripped the card about a
half-inch from the end and midway between
the sides with the tip of his second finger and
the ball of his thumb. The first finger held the
corner of the card so as to give it an added
spin when it was thrown. The actual throwing, that is the little snapping flick of the wrist,
Herrmann did in the same way as Thurston."

The author doubts that the explanation
would have provided much new competition
for Messrs. Herrmann and Thurston were
they alive when it was written. To add a

The Thurston Grip

The Herrmann Grip

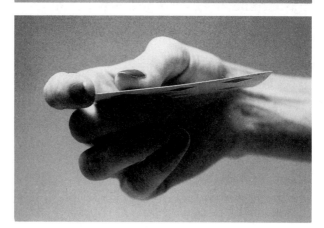

The Herrmann Grip (from underneath)

thought from the pellucid Jean-Eugene Robert-Houdin, known to conjurers the world over as the father of modern magic: "The performance of the sleight (to throw a card) depends on a certain knack by no means easy to explain in words."

The knack of which Robert-Houdin speaks is the wrist action as the card is released. The better accounts of card-throwing, those of Robert-Houdin in *Les Secrets de la Prestidigitation et de la Magie* (1868), Professor Hoffman in *Modern Magic* (1887), T. Nelson Downs in *The Art Of Magic* (1909), and Jean Hugard in *Hugard's Magic Monthly* (October, 1954) are all misleading on one salient point: the knack of releasing the card. Phrases like "jerk of the hand," "shot sharply forward," and "strong reverse twist" tend to make one think he is attacking an overall-clad clod rather than sailing a piece of paper.

T. Nelson Downs

The author has taken much time with the following explanation and has seen it work wonders. He believes his crowning achievement was in seeing a young woman, at that awkward age of fifteen, who in no way had exhibited expertise in physical or digital skills and who was not familiar with playing cards, upon reading the instructions once, sail a card with a perfect spiral some twenty feet to a wall and strike a picture of the author dead center, causing him pain and happiness simultaneously.

The keys to the incredible Jay method of card-throwing are two: the Jay grip, and the ability to relax.

1

2

3

The Jay Grip

First we must assume that the card, like the divinatory arrow mentioned earlier, can express four directions. The four corners of the card will now be designated as Northeast, Southeast, Northwest and Southwest.

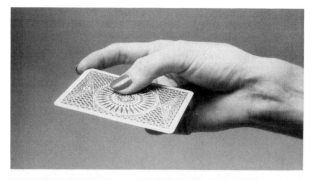

4

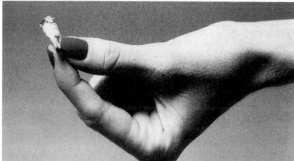

5

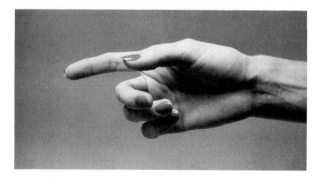

The hand as the card is released.

6

Place the Northeast corner of the card into the fleshy part of the right index finger tip.

The right second finger is placed under the card about one inch down from the index finger along the Eastern edge of the card. The right thumb is placed *over* the card in exactly the same position. The thumb and second

THE BASIC
JAY TECHNIQUE

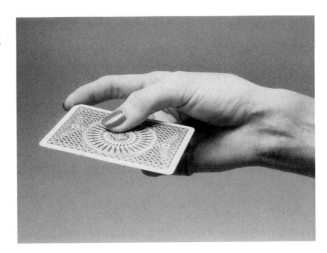

The Jay Grip

*The Jay Grip,
showing hand and
arm position*

finger have the card pinched between them. If
the cards were not present the position of
these fingers would be identical to that used in
passing the tiniest piece of cigarette to a close
friend.

The third and fourth fingers are kept out of
the way: this is most easily done by curling
them inward to touch the palm. The Eastern
edge of the card makes contact with the hand

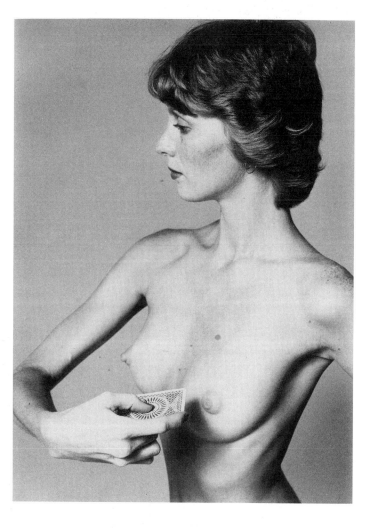

Cocking of the wrist before release

only where it is grasped by the first two fingers and thumb: the card does *not* touch the palm of the hand at this time. This is very important. Later, when the wrist is turned inward, the Southeast corner of the card will hit the base of the palm, but it does not do so yet.

You are now ready to learn the Jay throwing technique.

*Sit comfortably
in a chair.*

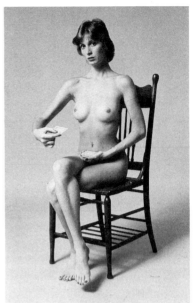

*Grasp card in Jay grip and
bend at the elbow.*

**The From-
the-Chair
Throwing
Technique**

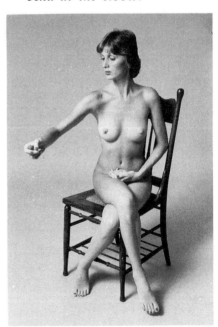

*Release and
follow-through.*

The basic spinning motion will be discussed first; the arm action for longer throws will be described later.

1. Sit comfortably in a chair (not an armchair). Your left hand, which holds the deck, rests in your lap.

2. Grasp a card in your right hand in the Jay grip. The right arm rests loosely against the right side of the body.

3. Bend the arm at the elbow so that the hand is now about six inches above your knee and parallel to the floor.

4. Bend your wrist towards your body until the Southeast corner of the card touches your hand at the base of the palm.

5. The wrist now straightens, returning to the original position, as the fingers release the card. The card glides out over the second finger, spins forward for a few inches (or feet), and falls to the floor. The motion of the wrist is the same as that employed in dismissing an incompetent valet.

After you get the feel of this motion you are ready to add arm action; this will provide greater stability and distance.

The Jay throwing technique with complete arm action

The entire throwing action is similar to that of scaling a Frisbee or saucer and the motion of the arm bending back at the elbow is like the swing of a pendulum. This back-and-forth action may be repeated a few times before the release of the card as a sort of warm-up

36 exercise; this is similar to practice-stroking before the shot in a game of billiards.

1. Resume the relaxed position in the chair. The chair will be familiar with you by this time and it too will be relaxed.

2. Hold the card in the Jay grip and straighten out the arm, keeping it parallel to the floor.

3. Keeping the arm in the same plane, bend the arm in at the elbow, back toward your body, at an angle of 90°.

4. The wrist continues to move back but the arm remains stationary until the card touches the base of the palm exactly as in the spinning exercise.

5. The wrist and arm swing forward to the original straight position and at this point the card is released.

6. The follow-through: as the card is released the wrist goes farther to the right of the extended straight arm and the fingers open slightly in a flicking motion.

How to throw a card and make it return to the hand, a simulacrum of the Australian boomerang. Also: fancy one-hand throws and catches for the serious student.

Advanced Technique

The most impressive stunt in the card-thrower's arsenal may be the flourish known as the "boomerang card." A card is tossed into the air for a distance of four or five feet. Suddenly the card seems to stop in mid-air, reverse direction, and return gracefully to the thrower's hand.

Though not as difficult or spectacular as some of the stunts you will read about later, it can be done with such sureness, certainty, and elan that it will impress all but the most calloused observers.

To learn this stunt, place the card to be thrown in the right hand in the Jay grip. The student should be standing in a comfortable position in a room with a high ceiling. Although the grip is identical and the throwing motion similar to that outlined in the last chapter, there are some new pointers which must be emphasized.

In the previous exercise you will recall that as the card was released from the hand the arm extended straight out from the shoulder and parallel to the floor.

To make a card return to the hand it is necessary to shoot the card *up* in the air rather than straight out on a horizontal plane. To accomplish this the arm must be bent back toward the face at an angle of about 45°; the card must also be sailed upward at a 45° angle. The fingers hold and release the card as in the throwing exercise, but there is a pronounced forward motion of the wrist as the card is released: it is this action which imparts the reverse-english necessary for the card to return to the hand. This motion is similar to that used in throwing a hula-hoop and having it return.

The Australian Boomerang

It is important to add that while the wrist *is*

Position for the Boomerang Card

snapped forward, excessive force is not necessary. In fact, a card may be thrown and returned to the hand with a very light and delicate toss.

A good practice exercise is to toss the cards very gently straight up in the air and catch them as they return. This helps to visualize the flight of the card. Next toss the cards out at a 45° angle and experiment with the wrist movement until you are able to make the cards return from a distance of four or five feet. With practice it is possible to propel the cards a distance of thirty feet or more and have them return unerringly to the thrower's hand.

When experimenting at the longer distances it is important to remember that how far a card may be boomeranged depends proportionately on how high the card may be thrown. It is best to practice in vacant auditoriums or the unoccupied high-ceilinged houses of the wealthy.

It looks pretty to catch a card at the fingertips but it is prettier still to see a card boomerang through the air and return to the center of a pack of cards. There are numerous methods of accomplishing this.

1. The easiest method is to boomerang a card with the right hand while holding the remainder of the deck palm up in front of you in the left. After the card leaves the right hand, the right hand grabs half of the pack from the left and remains poised three or four inches above the left hand. As the card returns to a position between the two halves, the hands quickly come together and capture the card in the center of the deck.

2. Place the deck well into the crotch of the left hand so that the thumb extends over the East side of the deck. The thumb curls around enough to grab about one-half the pack along this edge while the other fingers grab the remaining half from underneath. This allows the two halves to pivot open like a book and the card may be captured between them as it returns from the air. It is best to keep the deck closed until the last possible moment as it looks quite mysterious to see the card return to the center of an apparently closed pack of cards.

3. Again throw the card with the right hand and hold the pack with the left. After the card is thrown the right hand grabs the pack from the left hand, the thumb on the South end and the second, third, and fourth fingers grabbing the North end underneath the pack. The index finger is curled on top of the pack. The right hand now turns the pack around and the

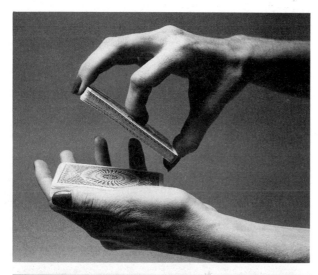

To catch a card returning to the deck. Method 1.

Card returns.

wrist is now rotated clockwise so that the thumb side faces forward. Use the index finger to press down on the top of the deck and the second, third, and fourth fingers to press up underneath. The cards are held

42 firmly in this position while the right thumb riffles down the end of the pack, opening it near the center and pulling it back toward the body. This leaves a hinge-like opening for the card to enter on its return flight.

To catch a card returning to the deck. Method 2.

To catch a card returning to the deck. Method 3.

Card returns.

It is possible with the following technique to place the entire deck in one hand and launch single cards forward from the top of the pack in a continuous fashion. Cards may also be boomeranged in this fashion and made to return to the center of the pack.

1. The Long-Distance Spinner

This is an excellent method invented by the late Audley Walsh and is adapted from the explanation in the *Tarbell Course In Magic* (Louis Tannen, New York, 1945).

The deck is held in the right hand with the thumb and second joint of the second finger holding the short ends of the deck. The index

The Long–Distance Spinner

finger is on the upper edge of the deck close to the right side. The third and fourth fingers are underneath the deck. The index finger presses down and the third finger presses up causing the cards to curve slightly because of this pressure. The right thumb presses its tip-end against the lower right-hand corner of the top card of the deck. The thumb must be held taut and straight with strong pressure. Without bending, the thumb snaps the top card upwards and to the right. The forefinger, acting as a pivot, causes the card to revolve in a clockwise direction.

The cards may be caught in the other hand, in a hat, or in the center of the pack.

To catch the card in the pack, refer to method 3 explained above. A simple modification from the throwing position will put the cards in the appropriate grip for the catch. As the card is released the third finger quickly moves from under the deck to take a position on the end next to the second finger. This leaves the deck held by the first finger and pinky with the second and third fingers merely lending support. After the card is released the index finger again curls against the back of the card; the hand is now turned palm up and the thumb riffles back half the pack exactly as explained earlier. The returning card is caught in the space between the packets.

2. The Martin Lewis Method

This is an exciting new technique. Hold the deck in the left hand between the thumb and second fingers at the Southwest and Northwest corners, respectively. The fleshy pads of the thumb and finger are pressed into the corners of the deck. The side of the index

*The Martin Lewis
Method*

*The Martin Lewis
Return to Deck*

finger pushes the top card down from the
Northwest corner until it buckles upward,
being pivoted against the thumb. The index
finger presses down about one-half inch,
further buckling the card, and then snaps
toward the crotch of the thumb. This frees the
corner of the card and it now shoots forward
and away from the thumb.

To catch the card as it returns to the deck requires repositioning of the left index finger. When the card is released the index finger straightens out and reaches over the top of the pack adjacent to the right side of the second finger. From that position the index finger pulls back about half the deck, hinging it at the thumb. The propelled card is allowed to fall into this space; the index finger lowers the top half of the pack, trapping the card in the center.

3. One Up, Two Back

A novel effect can be created by throwing a card into the air where it apparently splits into two cards; these return to the thrower, one being caught in each hand.

Of course two cards are scaled initially; these are held in perfect alignment in the Jay grip and then boomeranged out for a few feet. The cards are held together by the centrifugal force of the throw and its aerodynamic properties. As the cards are about to return they suddenly separate and are caught as described.

To make this stunt a little easier you may experiment with bending the corners of the cards. If the Southwest corner of the top card is bent up and the Southwest corner of the card beneath it bent down the cards may separate more easily.

The easiest way to separate cards in flight is to throw them so that they leave the hand already out of alignment. If the top card is slid one-quarter inch to the East of the card below it and the cards are thrown as described they will separate easily at the furthest point of the throw and return to the hands.

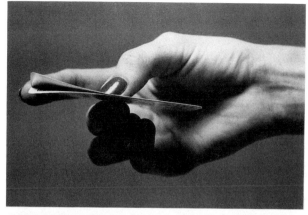

One up and two back. Method 1.

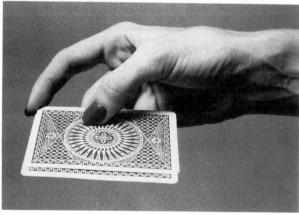

One up and two back. Method 2.

4. The Double Boomerang

A pretty flourish, virtually unknown in this country, was shown to the author by Finn Jon, the clever Norwegian conjurer.

Boomerang a card into the air and wait for it to return. Just prior to when the card would usually be caught by the right hand, the right wrist and hand turn sharply clockwise to bring the palm upward; the card is struck by

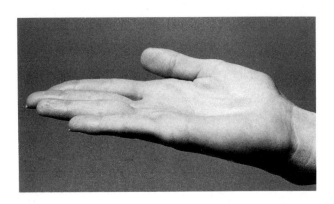

Back-of-the-Hand Flick

the palm of the right hand. This imparts additional spin which causes the card to fly out and once again boomerang back to the hand. The motion of the right hand and arm is almost identical to that used to impart back-spin to a Ping-Pong ball when hitting it with a paddle.

It is also possible to achieve a similar effect by having the returning card hit the hurler's elbow or wrist and fly out and back again. In all these variations the card has a tendency to veer toward the right on its second flight, so the card should be hit toward the left to compensate for this propensity.

5. The Finger-Flick

Cards may be propelled a considerable distance by flicking them with the second finger. The card to be flicked is held either singly in the left hand or protruding horizontally from the top of the deck as it is held in a dealing position. The second finger cocks up against the right thumb and then shoots forward hitting the Southeast corner of the card with the fingernail. The action is identical to one

used by most schoolchildren in propelling
expectorant spheres.

Holding the card or cards in the same position it is possible to shoot them forward by striking them with the unaided index finger or the back of the hand. This is a simple trick to accomplish but not nearly so pleasing as the finger-flick or butterfly swirl. Many hard objects may be used to propel the cards in a similar manner by striking the object smartly against the Southeast corner of the card. Experimentation will lead to strange and pleasing results.

Propelling card
with a pencil

The Finger-Flick

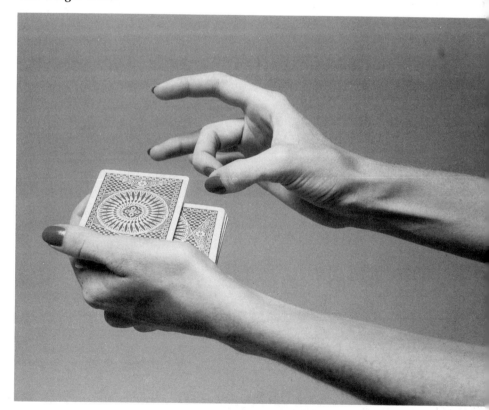

6. To juggle cards

To keep the cards in the air for a continuous juggling sequence is extremely difficult. In fact, the author knows of no other present-day performer attempting the effect with ordinary playing cards.

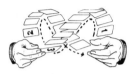

Juggling: The Cascade Pattern

There are three major difficulties in performing this feat: the cards must be tossed from both hands; there is no time to re-grip the cards for each new throw, they must be tossed immediately on being caught; and the cards are so light as to make it difficult to control their flight.

To master the stunt it is necessary to practice throws and catches without regripping the cards. This must be done with both hands. After these exercises are mastered you are ready to practice juggling.

Juggling: The Shower Pattern

The basic pattern to be used is called the Cascade. This consists of throwing the objects to be juggled under one another from hand to hand in a continuous pattern.

Place two cards in the right hand and one in the left. Softly toss a card from the right hand to a point in the air about one foot over the left hand and, before it falls into that hand, the card held in the left hand is thrown to a point one foot over the right hand. Before this card is caught in the right hand the third card is now thrown upward to occupy the same space previously occupied by the first thrown card. If you still have cards returning to your hands after a few tosses, you are juggling.

It is also possible to shower-juggle three cards. Showering is a juggling term for a continuous circle of juggled objects. Each card is thrown from the right hand and caught in the left in this exercise. Start with two cards in the right hand and one in the left. Toss a card into the air above the left hand from the right hand and immediately throw the second card in identical fashion. Before the first card falls into the left hand, the third card (the one originally in the left hand) is passed over to the now-empty right hand. As each ensuing card is caught in the left hand it is instantly passed to the right to be thrown out again.

7. Throwing cards with the feet

It is possible to sail cards from between one's toes.

The Foot Flick

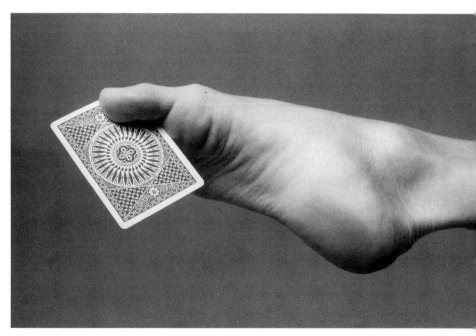

The hows and wheres of practice; techniques to keep the fingers limber and a short medical study of card-thrower's arm and its relationship to tennis elbow, surfer's knobs, and Frisbee finger.

6 ♣

6 ♥

6 ♠

6 ♦

How To Practice And Stay Fit

♦ 9

In any art, mastery comes only after diligent practice. Great instructors have stressed the importance of learning to practice correctly, lest untold hours be spent in inconsequential or even damaging exercises. How one practices is more important than how long one practices. Indeed, too much practice may have a deleterious effect on the student's physical and mental abilities.

Short practice sessions, not to exceed fifteen minutes at a time, are best. Two or three of these sessions will have a greater positive effect than a straight hour of work.

In addition, throwing a card involves musculature which is not generally used during one's daily activities. Too much practice in the early stages may be harmful. Caution is recommended to avoid injury.

The author refuses to take responsibility for the eager student who purchases this book and spends the next six or eight hours hurling cards at a photograph of Bill Bixby. Certainly, the author has sympathy for such excitement, but mark this warning well: it is not a wise practice.

It is as well to mention that the author refuses to accept responsibility for any personal injury the student may cause to himself or his fellow man.

Throwing cards is a potentially dangerous undertaking and each person must take the responsibility for his own actions. Although the author is a concerned, sympathetic, and emotional individual he refuses to feel guilty about monopedic casualties whose limbs were severed by a poorly directed toss of the card.

*German Military
Calisthenics*

Once the student has passed the beginning stages he may increase the length of his practice sessions, but please note that this is

not essential. Some masters of the art still use 55
the fifteen-minute plan with no regrets.

Before the cards are even touched, a period
of limbering and loosening is essential. Many
of the martial arts—dancing or yoga stretching
exercises—are excellent for this, but extra
emphasis on loosening the wrists, arms and
shoulders is important.

Masters of the exotic eastern disciplines
have frequently drawn upon animals to set
examples for human behavior. Yoga, kung fu
and karate all have exercises and forms based
on the particular movements of certain animals.

To acquire deadly accuracy with cards occasionally requires one to emulate animal pos-
tures. These may be used to assume the most
advantageous position for a shot, to limber up
before an assignment, or to scare an enemy
into immobility before an attack.

Loosening Up

Start with an old-fashioned finger pull. Com-
mencing with your favorite finger, pull it back
and forth several times; gently at first and
then with rigor. Repeat this process until all
the fingers have been pulled.

To loosen the wrist, arm and shoulder
simultaneously, one must adopt the attitude
of a young frigate bird.

Begin by letting the arms hang limply by
your sides. Start to slowly shake the arms,
wrists and hands. Raise the arms out, per-
pendicular to the elbows and continue the
shaking. Now lift the arms up high and shake
the shoulders, neck and head in a forward
and backward motion. Continue to do this

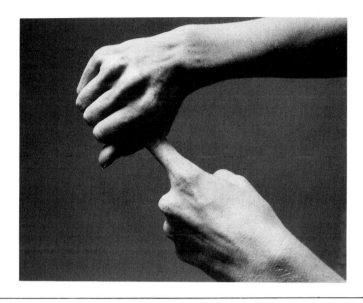

The Finger Pull

THE NEW YORK TIMES, TUESDAY, MAY 1, 1973

Tilt of the Heron's Neck Is Explained

By JOHN NOBLE WILFORD

Standing in the coastal shallows, its head and neck tilted at a sharp angle, the great blue heron appears to be listening to the wind or merely listing for want of anything better to do with a neck so long.

Actually, the pose is not idle, and two Canadian zoologists now believe they have figured out the primary reason why herons and some other wading birds often tilt their necks while standing or walking slowly through the water.

It is not simply a way of scanning the waters for fish, the researchers concluded, or of estimating distances between their sharp-pointed bills and the darting prey. The tilted neck would seem to be the heron's way of overcoming a problem familiar to any swimmer on a sunny day—the glare from sunlight reflected off the water's surface.

Heron Rates the Cover

The discovery was reported in the April 20 issue of Nature, a British journal, by John R. Krebs and

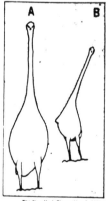

The New York Times/May 1, 1973
Head-on views of herons (a) on a cloudy day and (b) on a sunny day. In (b) the bird is tilting its head toward the sun to avoid glare.

Brian Partridge of the University of British Columbia's Institute of Animal Resource Ecology in Vancouver. A

sketch of head-tilting herons even rated the cover of the journal.

During the course of a study of the feeding behavior of the great blue heron along the Pacific coast of Canada last summer, Professor Krebs and Mr. Partridge, a student assistant, observed the bird's characteristic posture.

The long-legged heron, which stands about four feet tall and is often mistakenly called a crane, was seen holding its long neck at an angle for minutes at a time. Then, suddenly turning its head, it would strike at a fish.

The head-tilting occurred far more often on sunny days, the zoologists noted, and only when the heron was facing at an angle to the sun —that it, not directly toward or away from it. The observers reported that herons "almost invariably tilted their heads toward the sun."

Two possible explanations were raised.

First, fish may try to avoid predators by swimming out of the bird's shadow and toward the sun. Thus, over a time, herons may have learned to lean out toward the sun and cut off the

escape route. If that is true, herons should strike at fish most often immediately below their tilted heads—which the zoologists said is not the case.

Second, they considered a "glare hypothesis." If one stands in the water facing the sun at an angle, the sun creates a "patch of glare" on the water surface in its own direction. By moving their heads, the herons shifted the glare patch out of their line of vision without leaving a promising fishing area.

Professor Krebs and Mr. Partridge tested this theory by training a hand-raised heron to hunt for fish in an indoor pool. The "sun" was a 500-watt floodlight, the only source of light in the room.

The heron tilted its head in the direction of the floodlight. As the light was moved, the heron moved its head accordingly.

This led Professor Krebs and Mr. Partridge to the conclusion, as reported in Nature, that head-tilting seems related to glare and "presumably enhances the hunting efficiency" of herons in sunny weather.

rapidly making sure the wrists, hands, arms
and shoulders are limp and shaking loosely.

Rigorous loosening-up exercises are a deterrent to muscle-constrictions, cramps and soreness. Please do not let the fact that you feel like a ridiculous oversized chicken dissuade you from doing these exercises. In your heart you will know you're on the way to mastering the difficult aspect of the piratical frigate bird.

Next I will ask you to practice a particular swoop of the neck called the "Heron's tilt." (See *Times* article, p. 56.) This is a difficult procedure but necessary to avoid the direct rays of the sun which could ruin an important shot. The head and neck must be angled sharply to one side without changing the alignment of the throwing arm. The heron is able to keep this difficult position for minutes at a time, and with proper practice, human mastery of it is possible. This posture is especially helpful in avoiding glare on the surface of the water. The famous card-fishermen of Micronesia are particularly adept at this practice, and to watch them, sans sunglasses, pierce flying fish on a bright day in the Pacific is a joy to behold.

Once the body (yours) is warm and loose it is time to pick up the cards.

Practice Techniques

Set up a large hatbox in the center of the room and sit in a chair about five feet away. Hold the cards in your left hand and feed them one at a time into the right hand as you begin to throw. It is best to toss the cards lightly over the box so they will float gently down inside.

A Hatbox

58 This requires a subtle control which will be useful later in more difficult shots.

Once the student is proficient at this drill he should move the chair so that it is ten feet away, and throw cards into the hat instead of the box. I suggest a collapsible opera or top hat which may be carried easily, allowing the student to practice almost anywhere.

To throw cards into a hat requires a different knack than that used for target throws but it is a good stunt to practice for two reasons: first, it gives one a feeling of subtle control when it is mastered (note in the illustration how the wrist gently moves upward for the release of the card); and second, in the vernacular of the street, it allows one to "hustle a buck." True, the days when Rajah Raboid hustled the hatboys in the millinery shops on Broadway are gone, but a clever fellow can always get up a bet for cards-in-the-hat at the local barber shop or billiard parlor. If you're looking for an edge, if sheer skill isn't enough, then the following anecdote may be heartening.

The Eleven-Foot Shot

When I was just a tyke and card-in-the-hat and balkline billiards were big games, Ellis Stanyon was the Card-In-The-Hat champion of the British Isles. I was a cocky kid and not a bad hat man myself. I wangled a trip to England and set out to find the limey with the weird monicker. In those days, and things haven't changed much, the regulation hat pitch was ten feet. I found Stanyon's home court and cased it. Then I found Stanyon at the local pub and let him "hustle me" into a

Hats

game. The old-timers were trying hard not to
laugh at me, the little Yank they called me,
and one of the nicer ones told me to hold onto
my geetus and go home. I promptly told the
dude I'd go fifty pounds on the side: he took it
and so did a dozen other eggs.

To shorten the saw, me and the limey put
up a thousand apiece for a one-deck toss, best
out of thirty-two (that's all the cards they
used, those days) on his home court. We went
out back and old Ellis had just about the worst
day he ever had. First he tossed too short,
then too long, and by the time he was on I was
ahead to stay. I only nailed him by two cards
but that was just to make it look good.
Quicker than a flash I was back in Brooklyn.
Stanyon never did find out why he threw so
bad that day but here's the "G" on the joint:
before I ever laid eyes on the dude I found the
guy who set up the joint and I greased him
heavy to move the hat back to eleven feet.

I always thought I could beat the limey
straight, but I worked for a year on the eleven-
foot shot just to make sure. The mark never
knew what hit him.

Target Practice

These next drills are designed to have the
student strike a specific area with a card. First
find an old barn. Next find its broad side.
Stand six feet away and throw cards until you
can hit the side of the barn on every throw.
Mastery of this drill will enable the student to
win many a bet early in his career.

Now buy an easel and on it place a poster-
sized blowup made from a snapshot of some-

An Easel

60 one you dislike. Stand back ten feet and commence firing. After a few weeks, or when you are able to stick cards in the pockmark of your choice, move back a few feet and try again.

Though not a serious student of the occult the author is aware that it is thought possible to do bodily harm to an individual by hitting or pricking his photograph. This phenomenon would come under the heading of sympathetic magic as expressed by Frazer in *The Golden Bough*. It has also been called mimicry or imitative magic, and although most well-known with pins and dolls, modern-day sorcerers have been known to use photographs in these rituals. Indeed, many primitives still refuse to be photographed for this very reason.

Great care should be taken in this target exercise. It is not a joking matter; after all, this is a book on self-defense.

Long-Distance Practice

To throw a card long distances requires practice of a more direct and simple nature than the preceding accuracy drills. Distance throwing should proceed at the student's own rate and he should make sure he devotes at least one fifteen-minute time period to its mastery each day.

Starting indoors, you should throw cards with all your might until you can hit the farthest walls in your house. You then should move outside. Notice how much more difficult the scaling becomes. It is a good practice to match yourself against the elements when becoming a little too impressed with your own skill.

Careful attention must be given to the wind and to the pockets of air formed by the structure of the buildings where you practice. Change positions frequently until you can master the different airflow situations. Eventually you should be able to throw cards onto or over the roofs of small buildings. This is a sure sign of progress.

Medical Considerations

Long-distance throwing places a heavy strain on the arm, shoulder and elbow. Particular care must be taken to avoid injury or a condition known as tennis elbow is likely to occur. This phenomenon, called *teno-synovitis* by the knowledgeable, is also common to baseball pitchers. It occurs when there is an undue strain on the musculature in a specific area. The best defense against this discomfort and pain is warming up properly, and careful attention to one's daily practice habits. If this condition should occur, the best possible way

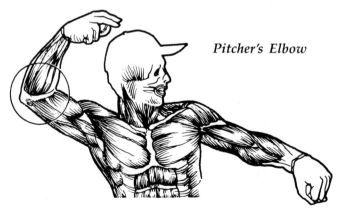

Pitcher's Elbow

to alleviate the pain is an application of the oriental panacea salve called Tiger Balm. It is available commercially in this country but I recommend a visit to the beautiful Tiger Balm Gardens in Hong Kong. An inferior American substitute called Cloverine Brand Salve may be found advertised on the backs of old comic books. One could turn a handsome profit or win a bicycle by selling this stuff to friends.

During the exercise called "drop and shoot," you start in a standing position; quickly drop to your knees and hurl a card. This technique is a must in the card thrower's bag of tricks and a vital defense against pygmy assassins. The sudden dropping to the floor may cause a bumpy lump to appear on the knees. This phenomenon, called *osseous callus* by the knowledgeable, is called "surfer's knobs" by the beach-blanket-Bingo set. It can be avoided by practicing on a rubber mat or wearing knee pads (see the advertisement for the special Jay model). If injury does occur I again recommend the application of the oriental panacea salve called Tiger Balm.

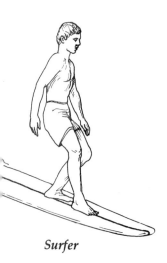

Surfer

Repetitive card-throwing may cause a scraping of the skin between the first and second fingers; this is likely to occur if the student uses the Thurston card throwing method. This scraping of the flesh produces a disturbance which is called "Frisbee finger" by the knowledgeable. The beach-blanket-Bingo set is not familiar with this term, and it may be used as a shibboleth to separate the men from the boys. If this condition does occur, it may be best to shroud the fingers with a clever western invention called the Band-Aid. Eventually a callus is built up on the sore spot. Switching to the Jay method of card-throwing, you're surer and safer.

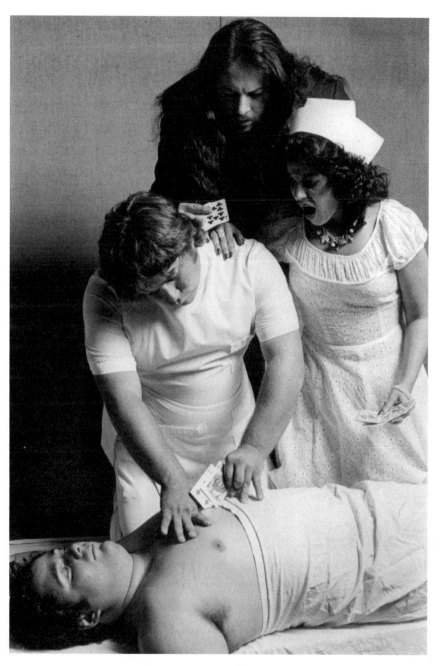

Emergency operating techniques using cards for the incision.

A prejudiced enquiry into the advantages of cards over more conventional weaponry. Special sections on self-defense against plastics and humans, and a pertinent discussion of cards as a pest control. Also, an added bonus: the secret fighting technique against multiple adversaries, the lethal "four card fist." And a second bonus: the consumer's guide to mechanical card-throwing.

Why defend oneself with playing cards? Indeed, why not? These are perilous, even parlous, times. It is no more plausible to go through life without thinking about defense than it is to forget one's morning ablutions. Yet, for most of us, the thought of striking another person—even to defend ourselves, our loved ones or our homes—is anathema.

In the light of this, let us discuss some of the important advantages of cards as a means of self-defense.

They are easy to carry, they are designed to fit comfortably in the hand, they are inexpensive, and they may provide countless hours of amusement before the actual encounter (if the student is a competent gamesman he may even acquire considerable fortune from his meager investment).

In addition, in these times when outraged citizens shout at police brutality and the restriction of constitutional rights, it is comforting to realize there are no recorded busts of persons carrying cards as concealed weapons.

Perhaps the greatest advantage of the card as a weapon is that it may be used primarily as a deterrent to crime and only in extreme cases used to maim and kill.

During the author's college days he worked as a disc jockey in a rather rowdy dance parlor. From his vantage point on a raised platform inscribed with the words "R.J. plays the tunes you wanna hear," the author had an excellent view of the entire bar and dance floor. Many times he saw an argument about to be transmuted into violence; as soon as a fist was raised to strike a blow, the author would hurl a card and strike the belligerent

Emmylou Harris defends herself against too-tenacious members of the Fourth Estate by firing a card from her guitar.

bozo squarely on the ear. The attacker, startled, would wheel around in search of the culprit. If his eyes did meet those of the author all he would see was the benign and innocent look described in the chapter on Advanced Techniques.

In this and many other situations the author has reduced a bellicose bonehead into a whining wimp with a perfectly accurate toss of the card. This invariably dissuaded such an ogre from his evil intentions. Some may argue that this is playing God or meddling where only divine intervention seems appropriate. While the author respects these feelings, his defense is that after years of study and the mastery of an art, one also acquires a sense of discretion applicable to most worldly situations.

A further moral note is appropriate. In carrying out self-defense techniques it is best to assume that one is locked in a life-and-death struggle even when practicing. Although human targets are the best practice material, they do not react well to such play-acting. Consequently the student may wish to provide himself with human effigies in the form of manikins or dolls, or a bevy of toy animals to serve as the objects of his attacks. (For information as to how this practice may be turned to more ominous purposes, see the discussion of sympathetic magic in the chapter on How To Practice and Stay Fit.) If the student feels it is important to protest the on-slaught of plastics, choosing a plastic object for a target allows him a subtle repudiation of society's polyethylene propensities. Although it is best to select nasty or malevolent crea-tures for this work, the author's favorite practice partner is a seemingly mild-mannered plastic duck. On an otherwise un-eventful carnival night in Rio this very duck took a piece of the writer's left buttock in its beak and paraded it triumphantly through the festive streets with mallard panache.

Basic Attack Stance

The Modern Playing Card Defense

It is with great pride that the author in-troduces this epochal system.

We will start with a discussion of the four basic throwing techniques for self-defense.

1. The Flick

This throw is used for its distracting effect and it is not meant to cause harm or do bodily injury.

Hold and throw the card as explained in the chapter on technique, releasing the card softly as you did in the practice throw. Should this card hit bare flesh it will cause only minor

annoyance but will serve as a warning and let
the enemy know you're Out There.

2. The Butterfly Swirl

This has a bit more bite than the preceding
throw. The grip is the same but the card
should be held with a lighter and gentler
touch. The index finger cocks against the
Northeast corner of the card and creates
enough resistance to create additional spin as
the card is released. The card will now travel
with more revolutions per second (rps) and
this produces greater impact as a surface is
struck. In the pain-tolerance tests conducted
at Duke University many people described the
reaction to the Butterfly Swirl with the word
aculeus which is defined as the bite of an
insect, hence the slogan "Float like a butterfly,
sting like a bee."

3. The Sea-Urchin Spin

The conventional grip is used but the card
must be thrown with added force which is
provided by the arm and shoulder. The arm
should be raised to an angle of almost 45° as it
crosses in front of the body prior to release.
When the hand releases the card there should
be a noticeable downward snap. The hand
and body must move together to make this
throw effective. When this technique is mastered this throw can produce a stinging,
pinching sensation, even against the Levi-clad
posterior of an adversary, and blood may be
drawn if bare flesh is struck. The pain inflicted
by this throw is likened to stepping on the
articulated spines of the edible sea-urchin

echinus esculentus found in the sublittoral zones of the British Isles.

This throw is critical in the mastery of self-defense. Though not lethal it can be very damaging around the eyes, throat and genitals, bothersome to the point of true annoyance at the mouth and ears.

4. The Dolphin Dart

The power of this throw has its analogue in the great driving force of the *tursiops truncatus* or common bottlenosed dolphin. The dolphin rams its opponent, the shark, at speeds in excess of thirty knots causing great internal injury to that predator. Using this technique, a card may be thrown with great speed and have a comparable effect on one's enemies.

For this throw the hand is almost straight overhead and the card held firmly in the standard grip. The right foot points straight ahead and the arm straightens in a forward direction snapping the card out at neck level in the same vertical plane as the extended foot. The card's flight should be such that a whirring sound is heard. This shot is very difficult and early attempts may cause the card to flutter to the ground at the thrower's feet. The release and snap must be timed correctly and the arm must move smoothly, though powerfully, at all times.

The Dolphin Dart is currently gaining popularity in this country, but for years was the favorite of Japan's Yakuza hit men. It is precise and reliable and should be used only in life-and-death struggles. In addition to the areas mentioned in the Sea-Urchin Spin, the Dolphin Dart is also effective at the temples, heart and kneecaps, and can paralyze a victim if it hits any vital pressure points (see chart) at close range.

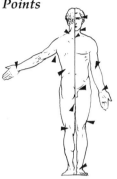

Special Techniques

1. The Children's Cudgel

The entire deck is used to jab and strike an opponent at close range in this exercise. With the right hand assume the familiar hitchhiker's posture, thumb extended and fingers curled in a loose fist. Place the deck into the hand so the fingers curl around the East side of the deck. Move the thumb down to the top of the deck and turn the wrist to the right so you are now looking at the back of your hand;

The Children's Cudgel

The Cudgel Grip

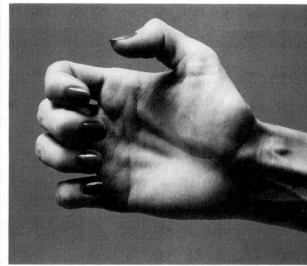

if your hand is large it may be impossible to see the cards from this position. This is a distinct advantage and gives you the additional advantage of the element of surprise. The cards should be gripped tightly and the blow may be delivered by shooting the arm stiffly to the right for a distance of no more than five or six inches. It is best to direct the cards against the knuckles, solar plexus, groin or head of an opponent. This technique finds its genesis in a sadistic children's game called "Knucks."

2. Round-Up

This full-deck technique both stings and confuses the enemy. Hold the deck in dealing position in the left hand, which should be relaxed. When you sense an enemy attack extend your right hand in the familiar handshake mode and surreptitiously lower the left hand. Quickly bring the left hand forward, hurling the entire deck at the face of your assailant, thus befuddling him.

3. The Lethal Four-Card Fist

This is the author's own defense against multiple adversaries. It was developed in New York but has a distinctly Oriental flavor and may be used in most geographical areas.

Place a card between the first and second fingers of the right hand, using the Thurston Grip explained in the chapter on Techniques. Next, place a card between the second and third fingers and then one between the third and fourth fingers; finally a card is placed on top of the index finger and secured by the gentle pressure of the thumb pressing down

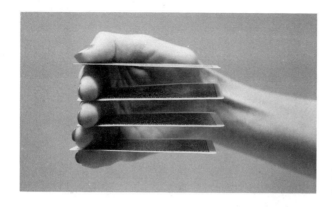

*The Lethal
Four-Card Fist*

against the top of the card. All the cards are held in the same relative position; looking down from above, one should see only the top card and not the three beneath it.

To fire, bring the right arm across the body and then extend it forward, releasing all four cards at once.

The cards will spread slightly on release; the top card goes to the left, the bottom card to the right. The two center cards will travel the farthest. With practice, one can strike four individuals simultaneously.

This technique is particularly useful in gang warfare and most effective when the user can throw with both hands. A skilled helper is required to load cards between the empty fingers of the person throwing. In this way two men can hold off a small army of foes.

Special Cards

Although the author uses ordinary playing cards for self-defense he has been questioned frequently about the effectiveness of poisoned, steel or razor-bladed cards. He has

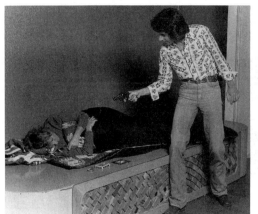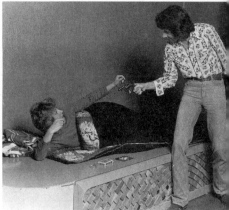

Self-defense to protect against a would-be mugger and/or rapist.

kept abreast of these developments in the field but is reluctant to make any recommendation.

There are, of course, certain advantages in the use of such products, but many difficulties may be encountered. First, one loses the disarming effect of simple paper. Second, the cost and acquisition of these specialized articles may be prohibitive. Third, the additional weight of these cards will affect the trajectory of the throw; the path of the card will be altered. It is possible to compensate for these disadvantages, but these are fiendish weapons which should be avoided by all but small children and those infirm of mind. Terrible tales could be told of one who practiced these deadly techniques and then inadvertently used the boomerang throw. . . .

Classes at
Columbia School
of Card Throwing

Classes at Famous Card Thrower's School

Self-Defense for Women

Although the basic techniques and practice exercises for men and women are the same, there are several advantages for women who become proficient in the use of cards as weapons.

Protection from the potential rapist or mugger is an essential in this society and no matter how unpleasant or distasteful this subject may be, every woman would be wise to at least consider the possibilities of such an uninvited advance.

In my women's classes at the Columbia School of Card Throwing, various attack situations are suggested and discussed. The problems are analyzed and the correct parries are provided. The more advanced students enjoy improvising responses and some novel and effective techniques have been found in this manner.

The Children's Cudgel (previously discussed on page 71) is a particularly exciting defense against the movie masher as it may be administered at close range and while seated. It is an effective blow delivered on the back of the hand, or, in response to more serious attacks, on the ear or under the bridge of the nose.

Many single card techniques are particularly useful against a masher or in situations where it would be awkward, clumsy or socially unacceptable to carry an entire deck. A single card jab to the neck or between the eye and cheek would be very effective, and yet not permanently damaging unless applied with unusual strength. A single card rolled up and thrust into a movie masher's nostril can be a fairly persuasive way of saying "no."

If you are accosted by a man who places his hand on your upper torso you may place one of your hands on top of his. When he relaxes, assuming this to be an encouraging response, you lock his hand against your body and use your free hand to push a single card under one of his fingernails and thrust firmly forward. This, embellished with appropriate verbal accompaniment, should make your attitude clear.

In more serious attacks where rape or even loss of life are at stake, blows should be administered with full force and directed to areas where they can do the most damage. It would be helpful to memorize the pressure point chart on page 71.

It is a wise habit to always carry cards in your pocket and/or purse, place them under the pillow at night or within easy reach at all times.

In the self-defense classes at my Famous Card Thrower's School, I may teach the rudiments of magic techniques which make it possible to conceal cards from view. The front and back palm is one such exercise. This may prove valuable if the attacker is aware of the use of cards as weapons. The cards may be hidden while in the pretended compliance stages noted above; then, when least expected, they can be retrieved and used for an effective blow.

Self-Defense for the Elderly

The abuses suffered by our senior citizens are now unfortunately commonplace; though frequently reported they are rarely dealt with in an effective way. While it is not in this author's power to change a society which has allowed such things to evolve, it is in his power to at least suggest some effective deterrents to theft or personal injury.

Cards are a particularly efficacious self-defense technique for the elderly because all old people play gin rummy. Consequently, cards are a familiar item and there is no need for long periods of getting acquainted with the product (like there might be with a crossbow or garrote) before effective results can be produced. Also, carrying cards may eliminate the need for the steel-plated-money-belt-and-undergarment combination so many of our senior citizens are being forced to wear for their own protection.

Forget the "you can't teach an old dog new tricks" attitude of so many people. I have demonstrated at the Columbia School of Card Throwing's Geriatric Classes that the elderly can learn to effectively throw and protect themselves with cards in only twice the time it takes a clumsy teenager.

Advanced geriatric coaching

Geriatric Self-Defense Class

Cards are among the lightest of weapons and should add very little burden to the shopping bag or pocket, and, of course, single card techniques are possible by all but the most infirm. An old person should never be without a card.

And just think of the social advantages of such a defense system. Upon being approached for any reason, the senior citizen can analyze the accoster and, if realizing he is a grandchild or otherwise harmless person, offer to play a little gin with him. Of course, it is always advisable to keep a joker at hand in case the newcomer is a poor loser, relative or not.

The Drop and Attack

This is an effective deterrent to robbery. If attacked, the old person should produce money on demand, securing a packet of cards secretly behind the bills. He kindly proffers the cards to the thief but at the last minute lets the bills fall to the ground. In deference to the elderly, the thief bends down to pick them up and the old person comes down sharply on the attacker's neck with the packet of cards in the Children's Cudgel position. If this technique is accompanied by the distinctive scream of the elderly, the thief—if he is able to move—will surely run away.

If an outdoor, non-contact prophylactic is needed, try this: At the approach of any unseemly character, our senior citizen should nonchalantly throw cards at a nearby tree, making them land firmly in the bark. He or she should then leer at the stranger who will hurry by or reverse direction.

Geriatric cases should not overlook "Cards

from Mouth" (the technique discussed on page 87, as it is a favorite of octogenarians.

Cards as a Pest Control

Ever since the publication of Rachel Carson's *The Silent Spring*, an alternative to chemical pesticides has been sought. Much attention has been given to protecting the environment and controlling industrial waste, yet the pesky fly remains a problem and the cockroach may outlast us all. In these times of Ban-the-Bomb and Back-to-Nature a personal combat approach may be the answer. If each of us slew his own weight in personal pests, we would solve the problem and simultaneously do ourselves honor on the field of battle.

There are, of course, some disadvantages in attacking insects with cards but this is to be expected of any solution. It really does require skill to strike all but the most lassitudinous specimens: this accounts for the wonderful feeling of accomplishment when the mission has been successfully completed. Furthermore, cards do cost money and if the edges crack or split upon contact with a hard surface such as the chitinous shells of an adversary, the cards become damaged and may not be used again. It may be far more practical to pluck flies from the air with chopsticks as Toshiro Mifune does in the *Samurai Trilogy*, as the chopsticks may be used over and over again. However, such a skill, though overwhelmingly impressive, is not likely to be readily mastered by Westerners.

It is best to start by attacking large crawling bugs, and then after considerable practice,

Chopsticks

A Bug

Toshiro Mifune

progressing by stages to small flying insects. You must pay careful attention to the moving target drills cited earlier; still, it is unlikely that you will have great success with animalcular samples. After all, this is not offered as a panacea for germ warfare.

Please keep in mind geographical distinction as well. Many a highly talented West Coast fly killer will swagger East to take on a New York City slicker and go back to California a bitter and broken man, finding the New York fly a much tougher character than his lethargic West Coast brother.

A final thought for the conscientious homemaker: take some cards and coat them with cinnamon mixed with four drops of rose water. The cards may then be strung creatively to form eye-pleasing mobiles and hung about the house. These are far more aesthetically efficacious than industrial pest strips and are environmentally sound; they are an effective deterrent to flying pests.

A Consumer's Guide to Mechanical Card-Throwing

There are no doubt some people who despite every good intention, frequent practice, and careful attention to detail, are too dysfunctional to master the Jay method of self-defense. This poses a serious problem. Can we allow these unfortunates to be abused by the hostile rowdies who inhabit our streets, and those who break into our homes? In all good conscience, we cannot.

For such people there are mechanical aids which, with a minimum of practice, may give a person a means of conquering fear and living a healthy and well-adjusted life.

A crossbow-like item called Zing-It, invented and marketed by R.A. Hamilton of New Jersey, is just such a device. The Zing-It consists of a T-shaped piece of wood about eleven inches long and five-and-a-quarter inches across at the bar of the T. A groove about one-quarter of an inch wide runs from front to rear in the exact center of the devise. A dowel of wood which is connected to a #64 industrial rubber band runs in the groove. The dowel is about an inch longer than the groove and has a projecting lug at its foremost end. The card is placed along the crossbar at the T where there are four pins to steady the card at the best angle for the shot. After placing the card in position, the dowel and consequently the elastic (which is connected to the underside of the crossbar) is pulled back with the right hand. The left hand steadies the machine, aim is taken, and the dowel is released; the lug hits the card, propelling it sharply forward.

With practice, one can become proficient at loading and firing with great accuracy and may reasonably expect to achieve thirty aimed shots per minute (spm).

Zing-It

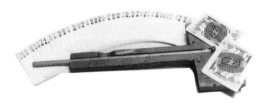

84   As a last resort, the solid construction of the device enables it to be used to bludgeon attackers at close range.

Zing-It may also be used for fun. It is possible to do the boomerang stunt with the device and also to launch paper airplanes. Mr. Hamilton's address is 978 Madison Avenue, Plainfield, New Jersey 07060.

An absolutely fiendish device used to propel playing cards was brought to the author's attention by Bradley Efron, the chairman of the statistics department of Stanford University. Professor Efron may have been the first person to experiment with the use of a regulation hunting slingshot to sail cards.

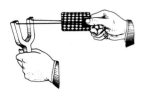

Card-Propelling Slingshot

The Wham-O Slingshot is recommended and available commercially at a reasonable price, but almost any brand will work. It is best to hold the slingshot with the left hand and the card with the right. The lower end of the card should be inserted in the pouch and held with the thumb and index finger. The left hand aims and the right hand pulls back and releases. The height, distance and speed of the cards propelled in this manner will exceed those thrown by hand by all but the most expert practitioners.

A strange device was used almost a hundred years ago by a well-known French conjurer named Buatier DeKolta. He housed a spring-loaded device in a bouquet of flowers; when a card was placed on the bouquet and the catch released the card was propelled a great distance. Using this remarkable contraption, DeKolta actually sent a card over the Flatiron Building in New York City. Though the actual details of its construction remain unpublished, those persons of mechanical aptitude are urged to experiment. Particular

Card Boomerang
(Wham-O)

Rubber-finger aid
to propelling cards

thought should be given to the engineering of card guns. (Please feel free to engage the author in correspondence if your efforts are successful.)

A strange device in the card-thrower's arsenal is mentioned in a 1949 issue of *The Phoenix* (a conjurer's periodical) by Audley Walsh. The product is a rubber finger, a device sold in stationery stores and used for the sorting of bills and papers and as a prophylactic for the first phalange of the employed digit.

Jacques Cousteau practicing the Jay grip in preparation for underwater self-defense.

The device can be used for techniques which call for a card to be shot off the deck under pressure (such as the Long-Distance Spinner mentioned in the chapter on Advanced Techniques). Place the rubber piece on the thumb or first finger (whichever propels the card in the method being used). You will notice that without any change in technique it is possible to spin the cards a much greater distance and with less effort. The device is also a great aid in fancy one-hand dealing.

Though shunned by the purist, this tool is worthy of investigation by the curious novice.

Underwater self-defense

For the Conscientious Objector

For those who would do no physical harm to
others even though it might mean the loss of
life or property to them, I suggest the venerable technique of "Cards from Mouth." The
pacifist, sensing danger, should secrete a
bunch of cards in the buccal cavity of the
mouth. When the attack is imminent and all
other options denied, he should quickly pull
the cards from the facial orifice. This will cause
the prospective assailant to gasp in horror and
run away. (Tests have shown the most un-
sightly combination to be one composed of a
mixture of court cards and jokers.)

An effective battery of crowd-pleasing demonstrations from the author's own repertoire. Included are award-winning throws such as: card over building, the classic card through newspaper, and the kudo-copping card-cuts-cigarette-in-mouth.

Stunts To Impress One's Friends

May I say right at the outset that a common failing in almost any profession and most certainly any art is a student's eagerness to propel himself forward at a rate of speed that is injurious to his ultimate advancement. I realize that many people have purchased this book with no other intent than to receive the tumultuous applause and jubilant congratulations of the multitudes after neatly severing the cigarette in a loved one's mouth or some other equally spectacular feat. However, I must hasten to warn that such things do not happen easily. There is nothing wrong in picturing yourself being carried off on the shoulders of a wildly cheering crowd after setting a new world's distance mark. Indeed, it is thoughts like these which inspire greatness, but let me add that in any sport there can be only *one* champion. It took me a long time to get there. Nevertheless, considering such things with a sense of the art and tremendous personal sacrifice, it no longer seems sporting of me to keep all the ammunition in my arsenal exclusively to myself. In a profession as hazardous as mine, there is no telling when or where tragedy may strike. To compound the tragedy of my own death with the death of an art I have worked a lifetime to advance would be more than anyone could reasonably be expected to bear.

Consequently, I am willing to release some of my pet secrets, some of the miraculous, original stunts that have been responsible for my international fame and personal fortune.

Reader, though many of these remarkable achievements will seem impossible, do not be discouraged. I assure you that with diligent practice each and every one of them may be

(*Left*)
Jay throws a card over Hollywood's world-famous Magic Castle for a prestigious panel of prestidigitators.

(*Right*)
Receiving the plaudits of the panel

realized. This will not happen in weeks, perhaps not in months, possibly not in years, but with the proper work and attitude, it can and will happen.

Needless to say, this chapter is not for the tyro or dilettante: and if they are wise, they will read it no longer. Such dabblers may skip over to a chapter stippled with funny pictures, and be amused. I hope I have not been unsuccessful in my attempt to give a little something for everyone. Serious students, are you with me? Good! Then I shall begin.

Almost all of the effects in this chapter are based on the acquisition of one particular skill: to toss a playing card with incredible accuracy. This may best be acquired with a daily routine of physical exercise and practice. I have out-lined much of this ritual in the chapter How To Practice and Stay Fit. I suggest that if you have only glossed over its contents you return to and reread it at once.

Ricky Jay and Mr. X, shown practicing at an early age

The specific technique for accuracy can, in its most mundane sense, be labeled target practice. I shall assume by now you have become proficient in the general areas outlined in the above-mentioned chapter and can successfully hurl cards through a swinging inner tube and toss cards into the designated cut of beef in the mock-up Jersey heifer.

The two new practice tricks which I am about to divulge for the first time should spur the student on to the mastery of some of the most difficult accomplishments in the art. Both of these techniques should be practiced with a trusted confidant or partner. For years the author practiced with a now-famous political figure noted for his blind ambition, who must unfortunately remain anonymous, but this is the perfect opportunity for the author to express publicly his heartfelt gratitude and thanks for the many unselfish hours that "Mr. X" gave of himself for the advancement of the art.

These two new practice drills can be divided into the areas of stationary and moving targets.

Stationary Targets

For this stationary target drill, first purchase a goodly quantity of a product called in this country "string cheese." This comes in a cigar-shaped stick and, once the protective covering has been removed, the cheese may be pulled apart in thin string-like strips. I particularly recommend the mozzarella as its consistency is best suited to our work. The Bordon brand with my picture on the package has been produced under the personal supervision of my staff and is consistently excellent for the job.

Bordon Brand of String Cheese

Have your partner stand in the center of a spacious room which has been first cleared of encumbering furniture. You should now stand six feet away from him. There should be indirect lighting both behind him and in front of you. This is important. Have your friend hold the cheese stick on his left hand and pull down the individual strips with his right. Each time he pulls down a strip he should fully extend his right hand away from his body and stop all movement.

You should stand in a relaxed manner, legs comfortably wide apart with the right foot pointed directly at his extended right arm (this, of course, if you are right-handed). The deck of cards is in your left hand and the cards are fed one at a time into your right after each release. You and your partner should establish a rhythm immediately. As he pulls the string cheese you simultaneously load the card from left to right hand. He extends his right arm, and about one second later you fire. It is best to aim directly for the center of the strip of cheese as this allows the most favorable latitude for your throw. The cheese pulling and throwing should be repeated rhythmically on every fourth beat for a series of thirteen repetitions. It is best to practice this for four sets with a minute pause in between. After the four sets stop to regroup the cards, get a new cheese, and repeat the process in its entirety. I suggest practicing to musical accompaniment, particularly something pleasing to the ear, yet with a monotonous beat.

This exercise can of course be made more difficult by the pulling of thinner strips of cheese, and with a greater distance between the partners. I suggest $1/24$th of an inch of cheese and one foot back every week until at a distance of fifteen feet a gossamer-like thread of cheese can be hit easily. The exercise must be practiced twice through, two or three times a day for maximum results.

Moving Targets

To hit a moving target requires considerably more skill than hitting a stationary object. There are, I suppose, some exceptions to the rule. Hitting a large stuffed toy panda which has been thrown into the air may be easier than splitting a piece of string cheese, but enough of humor and on to the business at hand.

In the past it has been difficult to find a target-propelling device which has more consistency than the human hand, but which

could also be regulated for height and speed.
A new product will solve this problem: the
revolutionary Ping-Pong gun. This is an air
rifle which shoots Ping-Pong balls easily and
effortlessly into the air where they can be shot
down by a well-delivered throw from the
student. While the Evel Knievel RemCo model is satisfactory I must, with no undue
modesty, recommend the Jay Autograph
Model Pong Missile Gun marketed by Ideallic.
The Jay model has a hand-controlled trajectory and comes with a set of luminous balls for
night work. It is a truly advanced product.
This is just a suggestion, and the cost of this
professional model may seem prohibitive to
some less fortunate readers. I do suggest,
however, that you look at the colorful advertisement, currently appearing in several na-
tional periodicals, before thinking about set-
tling for a cheap, second-best affair.

The Jay
Autograph Model
Pong Missile Gun

   Once you have purchased your pong rifle,
have your partner stand seven feet away from
you in a playground or yard. Do not—I
repeat, *do not*—attempt the practice exercise
indoors, as the popping sound of the ball
being released from the gun in an enclosed
area can cause permanent damage to the ear.
It is a good rule always to be careful when
using guns. Have your partner about seven
feet away from you and about six feet to your
left. He should hoist the rifle to his shoulder

Aesthetic combination of human and pasteboard forms

and fire shots first at about a 30° trajectory (setting #2 on the Jay Model), until he has released a round of balls. He should then increase the angle and, as in the previous exercise, as the student becomes proficient at hitting the target the distance as well may be increased.

The student should stand directly in front of the area where the ball is to be shot. He should have his feet parallel and pointing forward: his hands (deck in the left, individual cards in the right) down by his sides in the quick-draw position. He should then relax and give the command, "Pull," when ready.

As his partner next to him fires the ball he
should quickly sight the object and toss the
card. It is most important that the student
avoid thinking or speaking during this procedure. The sound of the gun firing may at first
seem like a distraction, but it is in fact a great
aid to concentration. Once the student is able
to block this earthshaking din from his conscious mind, he will no longer be troubled by
street noises or loud and obnoxious people
during actual test conditions.

The student should practice at least forty
rounds during the day and another twenty at
night. He should eat carrots and avoid tempu-
ra vegetables. Once he has mastered moving
target work he should get the Jay Mirror-Arm
Attachment. This is a device similar to the
side-view mirror on a 1958 T-Bird; the Jay
Model has special adapters which hook onto
the student's left shoulder. When the partner
shoots a ball the student, facing the opposite
direction of the shot, eyes the celluloid sphere
in the mirror and fires a card back over his
right side to intercept the ball in midair—a
difficult but impressive stunt.

One final word of advice: in practicing these
very difficult techniques it is important to
remember that the release of the card must be
precise and smooth. There should be no
jerking or pulling of the hand, but rather an
effortless and graceful spinning of the card. To
borrow an example from our Eastern friends:
one holds the card firmly, yet gently, like a
baby might hold the finger of an adult. One
releases the card like the baby might release
the adult's finger when suddenly distracted by
something else. If this convoluted Oriental
parable is difficult to follow, may I suggest a
practical Western experiment? Have a baby

98 hold your finger and then have your partner sneak up behind the child and fire the air rifle next to his ear. Notice how the baby impulsively, effortlessly, drops your finger and turns his head, his face grimacing in pain. This is precisely the way in which the card must be released.

In which the author recounts with clarity and excessive exaggeration how he has helped the elderly, abetted the police, and assuaged the plight of young damsels with the help of his trusty cards.

Personal Anecdotes

It was a damp chilly morning in late September. The click of the digital AM/FM clock radio and the alarming sounds of a big baritone sax had whipped me into sensibility. I hate coffee. Venice Beach in September is like a frightened woman.

I put on my floor-length terry cloth robe. It cost big bucks. I was thankful for the chill in the air which allowed me to use it. Smiling into the mirror, I washed my face and brushed my teeth. I looked silly with that toothpaste in my mouth but it put me in a good mood. I went outside to check the mail. There was none. Two pigeons were squabbling over a single piece of corn just in front of my door. I took a card from the secret marsupial pocket of my robe and maneuvered it into the Jay grip. It felt good. The first card of the morning always does. In a flash I fired the card in the direction of the startled birds. For an instant they fluttered their wings in confusion, but quickly settled down, each dancing possessively over a half of the kernel which the card had neatly severed. I took a big whiff of the ocean air and walked slowly back to the house. I was awake now.

Back inside, I plopped down in an overstuffed green chair. I put my legs up on the tea table; I hate coffee. I reached over to grab a book. It was a slim volume, W.E. Robinson's *Spirit Slate Writing and Kindred Phenomena*. I didn't understand much of it, but I loved the title.

I was reading about a dame who received supposedly psychic messages 'cause she had a telegraph key concealed in her hair. They had a picture of her. She was a doll. She had this telegraph key in her hair and a thread ran from the key to an overhead chandelier and

The Jay trophy room after a recent safari featuring the prize waterbok he felled with a single perfectly placed shot.

then down to an assistant who was hidden behind a curtain. By pulling on the thread the assistant could tap out messages to her. Suddenly the door bell rang. It scared the shit out of me.

I opened the door.

"You Mr. Jay?" a crater-faced kid in a Western Union bowler asked.

"No, I'm Mr. L," I said; I can really lay it on when someone scares me.

"Well," he said, "I got this telegram for a Mr. Jay."

"Give me the goods melon-head, I'm Jay."

I reached into my pocket to toke the bozo but I didn't have any change. I was still in my bathrobe.

"Wait a minute," I said. I stepped inside and found a four-bit piece. I tossed it to him and closed the door.

Damn kids.

I tore open the envelope and began to read:

MR. JAY
SERVICES NEEDED STOP MATTER MOST URGENT STOP CHEZ PUCE 9:00 TONIGHT STOP WEAR NIGHT BLOOMING CROCUS IN LEFT LAPEL STOP
SIGNED KARMI NOELL CO

Later that day I selected my boutonniere from Treppel's Florists and at 8:45 I hopped into my '57 Ford Sunliner and cruised down Pacific to Pico. The car was one of those wonderful old-timers, a slash-proof convertible with a retractable hard-top which lifted up like a yawning flamingo and then settled down into a cavernous trunk when you merely pushed a button on the dashboard. They only made them from '57 to '59. They were great. You could drive down the highway and wait for a couple of rubes to pull up behind you. Hit the button and the trunk flies open and the top peels off and you scare the hell out of them. Just great. A guy named Louis takes care of the machine. Does a fine job. He used to work on Bentleys before the war. The old Sunliner was in pretty rough shape when I got it to him, but now it was great. Cherry.

Just before Lincoln I hung a Ralph into a narrow parking lot and strolled into Chez Puce. It was nine on the button. The place was packed. I worked my way through the crowd and waved to Puce. She ignored me. I had no time to be insulted.

"Nice looking flower," said a dink in a pea green suit. "Care to join me?"

I had to think twice. It isn't often you see a dude suited up in this part of town in duds only Chuck Berry could get away with, but it was the crew-cut that really threw me, bad for the image; mine. He looked like a two-toned tortoise, but I could take a joke.

"Colonel Marki, I presume," I said as I took his hand.

It was his turn to gawk.

"How did you know?" he said in a thick voice accented with what a mooch would call German but which my professionally tuned ear recognized as High Dutch.

"The telegram," I said, "Karmi Noell Co., an anagram for you, Colonel Marki."

"I am impressed, Mr. Jay," the foreigner beady-eyed me. "I had no idea your expertise extended to these matters."

I could have told Marki that I grew up in the stuff. My grandfather was the cipher editor of *G-Man Magazine* for 14 years and I had accumulated an extensive library of cryptographic materials. I could have told him, but I didn't. I preferred inscrutability. My silence made him uncomfortable.

Still he paused, expecting me to say something. I watched the twitching of his lower lip. Eventually he interpreted my silence as meaning *your move, Marki.*

He took the bait.

"Listen Jay, this is a matter of international urgency and complete discretion is required. Officially, I am in Africa at this very moment."

I nodded, instantly catching his drift. He continued, "As you have no doubt heard my country is having certain problems with some of its neighbors who fall loosely into the category of 'emerging nations'."

"Hold on, Marki," I interrupted, "first crêpes, then conversation."

Puce made great ratatouille crêpes and fine French garlic pizza. I had toyed with the phrase, "First pizza, then palaver," but I had discarded it as inappropriate for the time and place. I filed it away for later use with a broad named Peggy who went in for that sort of stuff.

I hailed a pretty redhead wielding the tray that was the badge of her profession and ordered the ratatouille. Marki ordered one of those outlandish dessert crêpes with ice-cream, chocolate and almond syrup.

"Bring this immediately," he said abruptly and in a tone that stopped the girl in her tracks.

"Puce is not an octo-puce," I said, quoting by heart the aphorism printed in the menu. "Take your time, my friend."

The girl smiled her thanks and I patted her rear end as she trotted off. I thought of trying the "pizza, then palaver" line on her but quickly decided against it.

"As I was saying, Mr. Jay." Marki seemed irritated and frankly I enjoyed his discomfiture. He had a reputation for ruthlessness which I found appalling, but he was a very influential man, and I was tap city. The divorce had cost me a fortune.

"As I was saying, Mr. Jay, a picket fence does not always exclude a neighbor."

I complimented him on his use of the American idiom and let him continue.

"Three days from now there will be a clandestine meeting which shall be attended by very high-ranking representatives of the principal nations and another country which is peripherally involved. The tightest security measures will be taken and weapons are expressly forbidden. Nevertheless, it is my nature to expect the unexpected, and you, Mr. Jay, are likely to be the only person who could gain admittance to meeting rooms after a thorough frisking and still be fully armed and ready to deal with whatever problems may arise. Your services—" He stopped abruptly as the auburn-haired honey returned with our meals.

As she stooped down to serve the crêpe she exposed her proud young breasts which strained against her scoop-necked jersey like kittens trying to crawl out of a paper bag. As she straightened up, my hand, which I had cleverly allowed to hang limply just below the surface of the table, was treated to a ride along her smooth, pear shaped posterior.

"Will there be anything else?" she said, trying to hide the smile that her pouting lips could not conceal.

"Later, baby, later."

Karmi resumed in a half whisper, "Your services and your complete discretion are required. The terms are generous. Here is your plane ticket and a healthful advance." He dropped his napkin and as his hand reached under the table he proffered me a small package.

I had an incredible urge to pinch his knee and tell him I loved him but the divorce had really wiped me out. I put the gelt in my pocket and congratulated myself for having such control.

"Thanks for the meal, Karmi, I'll see ya in a couple of days." I got up quickly and started to leave. The redhead and I bumped into each other a few strides in front of the door. I whispered my address and she nodded quickly.

"My name's Valerie," she said.

"I'm . . ."

She stopped me abruptly. "Oh, everyone knows you, Mr. Jay."

"I'm Ricky," I said, "just Ricky."

Valerie and I had a swell time.

Thursday night at 11:00 I eased my Sunliner out of the sand and headed for LAX. My mind wandered; I was thinking about the beach one second, and the lilting tones of Prez on the car radio the next.

At Lincoln and Centinella I stopped for the red and looked out into the darkness. It always gave me the creeps that no one ever hung out on the streets in L.A. A night like this in the Big Apple would be buzzing with electricity. Here . . . nothing. The light seemed to last forever and the window of the school across the street stared at me like the eyes of a dying wino. I stepped on the gas.

L.A. International is a sprawling complex of

sheetmetal and aluminum. The eleventh most unsafe airport in the world.

I pulled up to the Japan Air Lines counter. I was booked on JAL's midnight flight to London and from there on a 17-hour British run to the end of the dark continent.

I had two bags. I checked one and carried the other confidently past the security guards to the X-ray machine. No trouble. I boarded the plane and took my seat.

I opened the suitcase and was greeted by the strange smiles of a gross of Tally-Ho number 9's from the U.S. Playing Card Company in Cincinnati. Private stock. A little thicker than usual. Precision cut edges. The real work.

I checked the lining of the suitcase I had specially designed to withstand the changing pressure on airplanes which so frequently causes cards to warp or bristle with a horrible cracking sound that drives me crazy. No problem now. I snapped the suitcase shut and placed it carefully under my seat.

I ordered a martini, very dry, from the kimono-clad cutie working first class. If she'd had tits, I'd have married her.

I looked around the lounge of the 747 and my eyes met those of a striking, stern-faced Oriental. We nodded to each other in silent recognition. Haruo Shimada, head of a notorious Yakuza clan, had been my employer for one of the most amazing exploits of my life some seven years earlier. For a moment my mind reeled with a pastiche of ceremonial swords, whirring cards, severed fingers, horned helmets, and pidgin English, but as my lips touched the chilled martini glass I eased into somnolence and before long

nodded into a well-needed and thought-free sleep.

When I awoke to the cow-like bleating of the loudspeaker, Shimada was gone, and the tail feather of a snow white dove was in his chair. I shuddered with pleasure and remorse at the secret Yakuza sign.

The plane was on descent and in a few minutes we landed in London's Heathrow Airport.

As I walked past a caravan of luggage filled pushcarts on my way to the British Airways counter, I heard footfalls which seemed to parody my own. Automatically I moved my right hand to my inside jacket pocket and eased a card into the Jay grip without breaking my stride. Boldly, quickly, impulsively, I wheeled around on one knee and fired the card at a blurred figure ten feet away. Midway between us the card hit another card coming from the opposite direction and both fluttered to the floor.

I looked up into the smiling face of Cy Endfield who ran forward and embraced me warmly.

"Just checking, Ricky," he grinned with the slightly warped glee of a mad scientist, and I found myself laughing heartily. "I still can't tell which of us fired first."

Endfield was the only other man in the world capable of such a stunt. Though American, he had lived in London for years. It had been almost a decade since our last meeting but he appeared unchanged. He could pass for a man of forty-five though he must have been sixty years old.

After a recent success with the invention of an interlocking chess set, Endfield had devoted himself to some secret electronics and

computer stuff but his life was crammed full of   *109*
unusual professions and incredible ideas that
spanned a half century.

I had asked him to meet me for two reasons.
Some years ago he had directed a wonderful
film on the Zulus and was an expert in African
military movements and weaponry. Secondly,
as a pioneer card hurler he developed a theory
that cards could be thrown with such velocity
that at the correct number of revolutions per
second they would emit a high-pitched hum-
ming noise that could kill a bird merely by
passing in front of it.

For years Endfield and I had corresponded
on this and other topics and I was anxious to
share his most recent discoveries. We spent
the two hour layover period in animated conversation interrupted only by peals of laugh-
ter. Finally, as I strode down the walkway to
the African bound jet, the wind snaked across
the tarmac and tugged at my trousers like an
insistent dwarf hooker. I turned to say good-
bye and thought I detected a tear on Endfield's
cheek. I wondered if I'd ever see him again.

I ordered a martini, very dry, from the
short-skirted cutie working first class. If her
legs were longer I'd have married her.

I looked around the lounge of the 747; I
recognized no one. For a brief moment my
mind reeled with a phantasmagoria of para-
noiac fears of the unknown but as my lips
touched the chilled martini glass I eased into
somnolence and before long nodded into a
well-needed and thought-free sleep.

I was awakened by the cow-like bleating of
the loudspeaker and dismayed to find we had
gone only as far as the Canary Islands. We
were herded from the plane like a bovine
conclave in search of nourishment. I might

have swooned with delight watching bikini-clad maidens on sparkling sandy beaches in the hot sun, but at 4:00 AM the airport employees, embittered by years of insignificant public service, did little to lift me from my somnambulistic stupor.

I was relieved to return to the plane. Sinking into my seat, I stared out the port and seemed to see in the plexiglass-shielded darkness the atavistic images of Mzilikazi and ShakaZulu conjured up by Endfield only a few hours before.

Little did those mighty warriors dream as they traversed the Transvaal, following the spoor of kudu and springbok, that soon their bones would lie beneath the windswept tarmac of Jan Smuts Airport, serving Johannesburg, the largest city in the southern hemisphere.

The airport was a twisted maze of queues and officials. I filled out my white and green sheets and got my passport and yellow health book ready and felt like a spiny lobster marching to the sea as I inched my way forward to the immigration and customs officers.

I thought of the unsettling television image of animated stick figures calling me "Alien" in squeaky voices, urging me to register at the post office every January or suffer a fate worse than death.

I had done my best to look like a tourist by wearing bermuda shorts and knee socks, and a thirty-five millimeter camera hung from my neck with the great moral weight of a sorority girl's lavaliere.

It worked. I was stopped only for an instant.

"Are you carrying any books or periodicals?" I was asked by a rosy-cheeked boy of twenty-five, all too proud of his sparkling clean white uniform.

"Not my style, chief." I saluted and walked on with not so much as a cursory glance to halt my progress.

I took a taxi to downtown Jo-Burg. The climate was pleasant, similar to L.A. but without the smog; the buildings looked down on me sorrowfully like lugubrious bushveld farmers trying to explain their presence. If the neon signs had read Hartford or Prudential instead of African Life I could have been in Newark, or Columbus, or any of a hundred big, boring American cities.

I checked into the totally pretentious Charlton Hotel where I was nearly attacked by a swarm of brown-uniformed, brown-skinned bellboys who seemed like a box of chocolate babies come to life.

"This way, master," said a middle-aged Bantu with a slight paunch.

"None of this master stuff with me," I said. And he nodded with no show of emotion.

I gave him a couple of rand, worth a bit more than a buck apiece, and I got to feeling like I was J.P. Morgan from the look in his eye.

"Put up the 'Do not disturb' sign when you leave, will ya?"

He nodded again and left without a word.

I took off all my clothes, slid a fresh pack of cards under the pillow, turned on the color television and began to read my complimentary copy of the *Rand Daily Mail*. On the TV, they were talking in Afrikaans and though I couldn't understand a word I found their jabbering relaxing in an odd sort of way. I thumbed past the front pages full of military movements and war casualties without pausing for a moment. The newspaper ritual was

POWELL.

similar to that of the television, the eyes scanning the pages but making no attempt to analyze or even register what they saw. I had long ago given up reading the sordid trash most people call "news." I stopped briefly on the entertainment pages and noted that Stephan Grappelli—the great jazz violinist—was in town, along with the Chinese Circus Revue of Taiwan and a Magic Spectacular at the Coliseum.

A knock on the door startled me. It's the same all over the world. You put a "Do not disturb" sign on the door and a minute later they're pounding on it.

"Who is it?" I growled.

"Special messenger, sir, sorry sir, very important, very sorry."

I opened the door a little way and exchanged a rand note for the proffered envelope.

The jerk was still saying *sorry* as I closed the door.

The envelopes contained my instructions from Colonel Marki, once again signed with the name Karmi Noell Co. No fiddle, acrobats or rabbits for me; I had exactly ninety minutes to get back to the airport and on a flight to Victoria Falls.

I hopped in the shower and let the water bounce off my back like hailstones off a window pane. I toweled off and got dressed in a three-piece leisure suit, open collared silk print shirt, and some high step demi-boots from Gucci. I had the vest especially tailored with card holsters in the side vents (an idea I adapted from the exploits of John Wesley Hardin). I carefully opened two new packs of cards, honed the edges to razor sharpness, and inserted them in the special vest holders.

I placed a few cards into each of my remaining jacket and pants pockets and then one card each into the two special clips inside the jacket at the armpits. With only a precise flick of the shoulder the cards would drop into the coat sleeves and down the arm into the hand.

I thought of taking the card crossbow which I could assemble from the sideflaps of my shoebox, but quickly decided against it. I also nixed the idea of steel-plated cards for fear of their clicking in the X-ray machines. It was just me and the pasteboards, but, I thought, it had been just me and the pasteboards many times before.

I took one last lingering look in the mirror; the three-piece leisure suit was a stroke of genius.

Two palookas were waiting for me in the lobby. *Marki's boys,* I thought, but I wasn't taking any chances. I drew a pack from my holster and tapped them on the table as if they were cigarettes. The two hoods approached.

"I'm Krull," said the shorter of the two, a little guy with pinched delicate features and a small pointed head. "He's Gerrada."

Gerrada looked like a cross between Ramon Novarro and Chester Morris. He was tall and reasonably built but not imposing in stature. He had a large nose and patent leather hair slicked back with some greasy pomade.

"We're from the Karmi Noell Co. and we'll be taking you to the airport."

"Thanks, boys," I said, giving the once-over to the Pinhead and Foodini team before returning the deck to my pocket. I wondered idly if I could see the future in the polished surface of Krull's skull.

The drive to the airport was uneventful. I peered out the window like some sap looking for lions or something but I had better odds of finding wildlife at the Polo Grounds.

We got on the Air-Rhodesia flight and the palookas told me Marki would be joining us at Bulawayo, about halfway between Jo-Burg and the Falls.

Marki boarded on schedule. He might have been entered in a Buster Crabbe lookalike contest—in his safari suit he seemed like an overgrown tyke in shorty pajamas.

Marki sat down across the aisle from me; the two palookas were a row behind us. A couple of mugs and a middle-aged woman got on, and we were off.

After a brief ascent the seat belt signs switched off and Krull kicked the back of my chair on his way to the john. As he returned, my neck twitched with that same uncomfortable feeling which accompanies the early stages of an hallucinogenic high or ergot poisoning. I turned. It was a second too late.

Gerrada had jumped to the front of the plane wielding a menacing Luger and I felt the cold hard steel of Krull's shiv kissing my neck.

"Nobody moves," shouted Gerrada who was facing the passengers in front of the cabin door. "We're making a little trip you didn't count on."

Men grumbled and women shrieked like a chorus of the Johnny Mann singers at the Hollywood Bowl. The cabin door opened and Gerrada smacked the emerging co-pilot without even turning to look at him. These two clowns were pros all right!

My mind was working overtime but the blade in my neck cramped my style; I decided to bide my time.

"Shut up, all of you," growled Gerrada.

"You," he shouted at the stewardess nearest the cockpit, "tell the captain of this rig to head for Uganda and don't try nothin' tricky."

The passengers had calmed down considerably and the plane started to wing on to its new course.

Krull had risen from behind me and worked his way into the aisle. Marki glared at him in a way that sent a shiver down my pant leg; for a moment I thought Marki was trying to put the whammy on Krull with those cold Arctic blue eyes.

"You don't scare me, Colonel," Krull said in a sibilant squeak.

"Why, you perverted little fool, you can't get away with this," Marki cried as he lunged for the palooka's throat with his massive mitts.

Marki had Krull by the scrag as the little guy tried to penetrate his thick Dutch hide with the point of the shiv.

"Gerrada, help," the pinhead gasped even as his blade cut through Marki's flesh.

Gerrada aimed the Luger at Marki and started to squeeze the trigger. In a split second I made my move. I twitched my shoulder and my eagerly awaiting hands received the prized projectiles of my profession. I fired the cards simultaneously. The right-hand card met the plump flesh of Gerrada's neck with a muted thwack and a thin almost imperceptible line of blood appeared. The left-hand card hit the wrist but a fraction of a second too late. The gun blared out its awful din before falling to the floor only a moment before Gerrada himself.

The deflected bullet flew past its intended victim and cracked the window beside the still-entwined and struggling bodies of Krull and Marki.

As the glass cracked it was as if the entire world swept into the giant tornado that took Dorothy from Kansas to Oz. The oxygen masks dropped out of their overhead holders like victims at a mass execution. The windows covered with mist and the hot African sun faded from view. Coffee cups, serving carts, pillows, knives, spoons and magazines bounced around like popcorn on a stove. Then, in a maze of arms and legs and screams, Marki and Krull were drawn to the open window. They struggled together with a unity so characteristic of the human species in times of stress. I watched them grope and twist and grasp for footing like cats on a pane of glass, but to no avail; with a giant woosh and a horrible harmonious groan they were sucked through the window into the giant vacuum cleaner of the sky.

The pilot crash-dove to eight thousand feet to get breathable air as the frightened passengers heaved and coughed and cried and fainted in their seats. The stewardesses were clinging to the steel handles in the serving sections for dear life and Gerrada was saved from the horrible flying fate of his partner only because his bleeding hulk was jammed into the passageway between the cockpit and cabin.

The hurricane was dying down now and the pilot was announcing a landing in a clearing a few minutes away. I cupped my ears with my hands to drown out the frightening cacophony of the human voice in fear; as I looked from the plane I saw a huge body of zebras and wildebeest scatter in a kaleidoscopic whirl as the plane, like an injured red hornbill, approached the savannah that was to be its final resting place. As the jet hit the

Stanley, Livingstone, and the Victoria Falls

ground and thumped along like a giant juggler's mistake, I lost consciousness.

Victoria Falls. MOSI OA TUNYA. The smoke that thunders. 38,430 cubic feet of water per second. Dr. Livingstone I presume. What's the question? Gertrude Stein. Spencer Tracy. Richard Burton. Alan Moorehead.

118   I dreamt a storm of magnificent proportions and when I awoke I still heard thunder though the sky was cloudless and bright. As I wiped my eyes and turned towards the noise I saw a strange smokey mist swirl beneath a magnificent crowning rainbow. I kicked out the exit door on the wing and crawled towards what I realized was Victoria Falls, driven by some impulse kindled in recesses far beneath my conscious mind. In the distance I heard the sirens of the rescue vehicles but I didn't even stop to turn around. I plodded along on my strange mission like a lemming on his way to the cliffs. Sure, I got to the Falls.

But that is another story.

A sad footnote. The death by suicide of a San Quentin inmate who blew himself to a netherworld with a bomb fashioned from a pack of cards. For those who doubt the seriousness of the subject or the tone of the tome.

Afterword

*Jiggs the
Actor/Chimpanzee*

It seems appropriate to end this documented account of cards as weapons with a story that has been deemed worthy of entry in the legendary *Ripley's Believe It Or Not*.

The author has wended his way through reels of microfilm of 1930's newspapers (enough to know the names of the "human notables" present at the funeral of Jiggs the famous actor/champanzee) in an attempt to find the original article. This proved a futile endeavor. The only other reference to this remarkable anomaly appeared in the April 1938 issue of a long-defunct magic periodical called *The Jinx*.

The Jinx was edited by the amazing wunderkind of mental magic, Theodore Annemann. This is his account:

"In San Quentin a supposedly ignorant prisoner blew himself to bits with a pack of ordinary playing cards. Cards are made of cellulose from which a powerful explosive, trinitro-cellulose, is made. The condemned man scraped only the red spots from the pack, soaked the pieces thoroughly, and crammed them into a hollow pipe taken from his cot. Heated over a small oil lamp the crude bomb exploded and tore the prisoner to shreds."

Mr. Annemann's sagacious advice to the magic fraternity was, "Brother, don't drop that deck!"

A Sad Footnote to a Sad Footnote

Annemann was considered a strange figure in magic and, by all but a few, he was thought a genius in the methods of duplicating psychic or mental phenomena; he was a creative

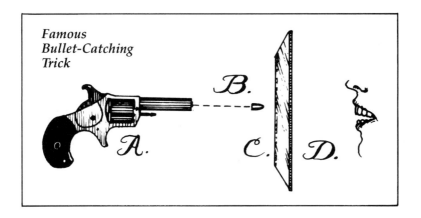

Famous Bullet-Catching Trick

thinker but always a reluctant and nervous performer. It was big news when advertisements for his full evening show appeared in the New York press. Annemann was to appear at "The Little Theatre in the Sky" atop the Chanin Building on New York's 42nd Street on January 26th and 27th, 1942.

The feature of the show was to be the famous Bullet-Catching Trick. A committee purchased, examined and marked a bullet which was then loaded into a rifle belonging to a spectator, a marksman, who had never met the performer. The marksman hoisted the rifle to his shoulder and took aim at the mouth of the performer who stood blindfolded on the opposite side of the stage with his hands behind his back. The commands, "Ready—Aim—Fire!" were given. A shot rang out and the performer dropped to his knees; there was a trickle of blood from the corner of his mouth and then miraculously the marked bullet was seen to emerge from between his lips.

Over the years twelve magicians had lost their lives presenting this spectacular effect, and the magic fraternity spoke of the upcom-

ing Annemann attempt with strained antici-
pation.

It is easy to speculate that Annemann, too,
felt the strain, not only of this trick and this
show but of the other confused pieces of his
life. He did not do the performance. On
January 12th, a few miles away from the
theatre, he locked himself in his room and
committed suicide.

My grandfather was to be the producer of
the Annemann show.

I mention this in case Kurt Vonnegut is
planning another novel.

A Strange Footnote to a Sad Footnote

Recently, while reposing in the Las Vegas
home of The Great Tomsoni, Poland's entry
into the world of sophisticated sorcery and the
star of the Folies-Bergère revue at the Tropica-
na Hotel, I happened upon a copy of Irving
Wallace's *The Fan Club*.

I read the back cover blurb:

> "The Plan: to capture her and teach her
> the realities of love.
> The Act: a bold kidnaping of the world's
> Number One sex symbol.
> The Climax: the American dream of per-
> fect love turns into a shattering night-
> mare of lust and terror."
>
> ("Possibly the best thing he's done yet"—
> *New York Times Syndicate*)*

---

*This seems rather severe criticism.

The Great Tomsoni

My mood was such that I devoured the book greedily, drooling over the abduction and subsequent ill-use of the sultry movie star. I could not help thinking that if the lovely damsel had only a deck of cards and had read this book how easily she could have delivered herself from the hands of her savage captors by using the "Lethal Four-Card Fist" described on page 72.

But such was not the case. The heroine was incarcerated by the cruel coterie and there seemed to be no way out. To quote Mr. Wallace:

"Yes, she was caged, trapped, with as much chance of escape as a prisoner locked in solitary confinement inside San Quentin.

"San Quentin? What had made her think of that one-time high security California penitentiary?"

What? What indeed!

Quickly we find out:

"She had total recall, and recall had brought it back to her."

We can presume that total recall is a common enough attribute of sex-symbol movie stars.

And now, with the ease of Marlin Perkins sliding from the protection a mother sloth gives her young to the protection you can receive from Mutual of Omaha, Wallace segues to the suicide of a San Quentin inmate with a deck of cards.

And so it is here, in this Irving Wallace classic, that I find the missing pieces of the puzzle and the end to my strange tale.

The man's name is William Kogut. He is a lumberjack. Sentenced to death for murdering a woman, he vows that he will never be put to death by the state.

As his final day draws near he conceives his devious plan. He scrapes and soaks the red pips of the cards and stuffs them into the leg of his cot with a broom handle; the broom handle is left in the tubing to make it airtight. He holds the makeshift bomb over the flame of the oil lamp all night and finally, as morning arrives and the gas pressure builds up sufficiently, Kogut's efforts are rewarded with translation to a more tolerable plane of existence.

Facts, names, motives—all clearly before me in cold print; and then, one final gem.

Mr. Wallace mentions—and I applaud his restraint and subtlety—Mr. Wallace mentions, in no uncertain terms, that this man who blew himself to bits with the ultimate pasteboard pyrotechnic, was Polish.

Marlin Perkins

Map of Poland

Fastest
Gun In
The
West

ACKNOWLEDGMENTS

With this book comes a long line of friends who have offered the author a helping appendage, typewriter or money and who should be acknowledged publicly no matter how much this may jeopardize their individual careers.

First, to T.A. Waters, good friend, prolific author, and eminent psychologician, who spent so much time and energy on this project it almost seemed he was living in my house. There is little doubt I would have been unable to finish this book without his help. His penchant for philogistic phraseology has been a constant inspiration.

To Dennis Plehn and Bruce Ayres for shooting and organizing the many photographs and to those splendid souls who arranged for or appeared as subjects in them: Wendy Summers, BBC-TV, John Fisher, Michael Parkinson and staff, Emmylou Harris, the Getz-Tichner Organization, John Zehnder, Norris McWhirter, Carl Sagan, Andrew Solt, Dai Vernon, Joe Cossari, Don Lawton and the exciting Los Angeles–based theatre company, the Groundlings.

To John Dean, my kinky friend, for suggestions which greatly enhanced this volume, to Mo for the chicken wings, and Ron Popeil for the intro.

To Charles and Regina Reynolds for their elan and for introducing me to my publisher Jack Rennert, who, along with his faithful colleagues Jane Wagner and Helen Garfinkle and Darien House staff members Stu Solow and Valerie Beale, provided me with a most unusual experience and a wonderful time in New York.

To the staff and members of the Magic 129
Castle for permitting me to enter their hallowed halls and make use of their excellent library. To the Library of Congress and special collections curator Leonard Beck for gracious help in my research. To Jay Marshall, that Midwestern master of mirth, mystery and minutia, for the use of the rare left-handed magicians' throwing cards from his collection. To Milbourne Christopher, well-known magic historian and the only Caucasian member of the All-India Magic Society, for information on Buatier de Kolta; though long since dead, vitally important to this book. To Martin Lewis, Finn Jon, and Flip for allowing me to include previously unpublished original material.

To Stuart Gordon for barristering, bantering and bargaining on my behalf.

To Deborah Baron for unsolicited testimony beyond the call of guilt or friendship.

To Karen Hitzig for advice in heavy times, to Candace Lake for her candor and kudu.

To Chuck Fayne—if you need anything call him. I did, frequently.

To Lindley R. Armitage, a fascinating gentleman, for his important advice on body dynamics.

To Charles Miller, Dai Vernon, Pete Biro, Pat Page, Bruce Cervon, Michael Perovich, Cy Endfield, Haruo Shimada, Bill Liles, Scott York, John Thompson and Derek Dingle, for being sounding boards, suggesters, and too good to be called magicians.

To Steve Freeman, mon frère Isola for his elegant touch.

To Professor Dr. Well, for yet another possibility . . .

To Valerie Farnum, Tracy Newman, Alex

130 Lange, Spencer Troy and McCabes Guitar Shop for less specific but no less important help.

To Itto Ogami for the seagull wave slash technique.

Special thanks to Gary Cooley for his absolutely wonderful cover art. Border art is by Michael Gregory. Production was under the capable supervision of Andrew Merson, Gary Feller and Dave Miller.

Unless otherwise credited, all photographs were meticulously taken by Dennis Plehn. Playing cards were photographed by Robert Koch. Photos taken at BBC-TV Center in London, reproduced on pages 15-16 are by Dave Edwards and used by kind permission of BBC. The article on page 56 is reproduced from *The New York Times* and is copyright 1973 by The New York Times Company. The Card Boomerang featured on page 85 is manufactured by the Wham-O Mfg. Co., San Gabriel, California. The Crazy Horse Saloon in Malibu, California and the Israel Levin Center in Venice, California provided hospitality to the author. To all these people and companies, my sincere thanks.

And, finally, but I hope not, to Bozo.

—**Ricky Jay**
Venice, California
March 1977